# Privacy:
# The Impact of ARRA, HITECH, and Other Policy Initiatives

Jill Callahan Dennis, JD, RHIA

Copyright ©2010 by the American Health Information Management Association. All rights reserved. No part of this publication may be reproduced, stored in a retrieval system, or transmitted, in any form or by any means, electronic, photocopying, recording, or otherwise, without the prior written permission of the publisher.

ISBN: 978-1-58426-253-4

AHIMA Product Number: AB101710

AHIMA Staff:
Claire Blondeau, MBA, Senior Editor
Angela K. Dinh, MHA, RHIA, CHPS Technical Review
Katie Greenock, Editorial and Production Coordinator
Beth Hjort, RHIA, CHPS, Technical Review
Ashley Sullivan, Assistant Editor
Pamela Woolf, Developmental Editor
Ken Zielske, Director of Publications

The Web sites listed in this book were current and valid as of the date of publication. However, Web page addresses and the information on them may change or disappear at any time and for any number of reasons. The user is encouraged to perform his or her own general Web searches to locate any site addresses listed here that are no longer valid.

This publication is designed to provide accurate and authoritative information in regard to the subject matter covered. It is sold with the understanding that the publisher is not engaged in rendering legal, accounting, or other professional services. If legal advice or other expert assistance is required, the service of a competent professional person should be sought.

All products mentioned in this book are either trademarks of the companies referenced in this book, registered trademarks of the companies of the companies referenced in this book, or neither.

American Health Information Management Association
233 North Michigan Avenue, 21st floor
Chicago, Illinois 60601
ahima.org

# Contents

About the Author .................................................................................................v
Preface ................................................................................................................vii
Acknowledgments ...............................................................................................ix
Foreword .............................................................................................................xi
How to Use This Book ......................................................................................xiii

**Chapter 1**   **Overview of the American Recovery and Reinvestment Act of 2009's HITECH Provisions** ........................................................1
    The Need for Legislation and Regulation ................................................1
    ARRA ........................................................................................................3
        Affected Parties ..................................................................................5
    The Big Picture .........................................................................................6

**Chapter 2**   **Key Provisions Impacting the HIPAA Privacy Rules** ....................9
    Codification of ONC and ONC Duties ................................................10
    Key Business Associate Provisions .........................................................11
    Breach Notification Provisions ..............................................................19
    Requests for Restrictions on Certain Disclosures ..................................24
    Restrictions on the Sale of Health Information ....................................25
    Right to Access in Electronic Form .......................................................25
    Accounting of Disclosures .....................................................................26
    Minimum Necessary and the Limited Data Set ....................................27
    New Conditions for Marketing and Fundraising Contacts ...................28
    Enforcement Provisions .........................................................................30
    Important Provisions for Noncovered Entities ......................................31
    Education on Health Information Privacy ............................................32

**Chapter 3**   **Operational Challenges** .................................................................35
    Who Needs to Know What ...................................................................35
    The Rules Are a Moving Target .............................................................37
    Breaches Will Be Numerous ..................................................................39
    The Need for New or Revised Policies and Procedures .........................40

|  |  |  |
|---|---|---|
|  | Business Associate Agreement Revisions | 41 |
|  | Ongoing Challenges with Preemption Analysis | 42 |
| **Chapter 4** | **Implementation Strategies** | **43** |
|  | Implementing Change | 44 |
|  | Guide the Change Process | 44 |
|  | Divide Up the Work | 45 |
|  | Set Priorities | 45 |
| **Chapter 5** | **Impact beyond the HIPAA Privacy and Security Rules** | **51** |
|  | State Laws | 51 |
|  | The Role of the Federal Trade Commission | 51 |
|  | State Attorneys General and Civil Actions | 54 |
|  | Impact on EHR Availability | 54 |
| **Chapter 6** | **Unresolved Questions and Conflicts** | **55** |
|  | State Breach Notification Laws | 55 |
|  | Defining Breach | 56 |
|  | Breach Exceptions | 58 |
|  | Business Associate Agreements | 59 |
| **Chapter 7** | **Policy Efforts Impacting the Privacy Rules of ARRA** | **61** |
|  | The Nationwide Privacy and Security Framework | 61 |
|  | Growing Role of the Federal Trade Commission | 72 |
|  | ONC's HIT Policy Committee | 73 |
|  | eHealth Initiative Blueprint: Principles on Managing Privacy, Security, and Confidentiality | 83 |
|  | The Markle Foundation's Connecting for Health Project | 84 |
|  | Other Organizations and Collaborations | 86 |
| **Appendix A** | **Frequently Asked Questions (FAQs)** | **89** |
|  | General Questions | 89 |
|  | Breaches | 91 |
|  | Accounting of Disclosures | 92 |
|  | Patient Rights and Requests | 93 |
|  | Business Associates and Business Associate Agreements | 94 |
|  | Staff Education | 95 |
| **Index** |  | **97** |

**On the CD-ROM**

Appendix B: Web Resources (with Links)
Appendix C: ARRA's Final Law (PDF)
Appendix D: HHS Breach Regulations 8/2009 (PDF)
Appendix E: Federal Trade Commission Health Breach Notification Rule 8/2009 (PDF)

# About the Author

**Jill Callahan Dennis, JD, RHIA** is principal of Health Risk Advantage, a Colorado-based risk management consulting firm that assists healthcare organizations to minimize their risk of liability. Prior to this, she was senior vice president, public and industry leadership for the American Health Information Management Association (AHIMA), where she helped plan and execute the association's policy and alliance agendas. Her leadership on health information management issues spans almost 30 years, and she is a frequent speaker on risk management, privacy, and electronic health information management topics. Her publications include numerous articles, chapter author of "Legal Issues in Health Information Management" in *Health Information: Management of a Strategic Resource*, by Abdelhak, et.al. (Elsevier 2007), author of the book *Privacy & Confidentiality of Health Information* (Jossey-Bass and AHA Press 2000), and technical editor of *HIPAA by Example* (AHIMA 2007). Jill served on AHIMA's Board of Directors from 2002 through 2007 and as the elected president in 2006. She was a member of the Confidentiality, Privacy, and Security Workgroup of the American Health Information Community (AHIC) of the U.S. Department of Health and Human Services' Office of the National Coordinator for Health Information Technology. She has a law degree from Loyola University of Chicago, a master's in administration (health administration concentration) from Central Michigan University, and a bachelor of science degree in medical record administration from Ferris State University.

# Preface

On February 17, 2009, President Obama signed the American Recovery and Reinvestment Act of 2009 (ARRA) into law. ARRA's language creates some interesting new questions for those working in the health information privacy arena. This book explores those questions. The advice here is not intended as legal advice, but rather as a guide to some of the issues and questions one will encounter while implementing the health information privacy and security provisions of ARRA. Key provisions of the legislation, unanswered questions, likely operational challenges, and possible implementation strategies are covered, along with an overview of some of the other privacy- and security-related policy efforts now underway.

Privacy and security compliance is not a one-time event. It is a journey that never ends. I hope this book will help you along the way. It is written for the countless professionals that do their best, day after day, year after year, to safeguard patients' health information while pursuing a vision of quality healthcare through quality information.

—Jill Callahan Dennis, JD, RHIA

# Acknowledgments

There isn't a more supportive publishing team around than the Publications crew at AHIMA. Special thanks to Pamela Woolf for the great advice on ways to make the book clearer and more useful, and to Angela Dinh and Beth Hjort of the Practice Resources staff for the insightful technical reviews. I'm grateful to Claire Blondeau for the invitation to write. Dan Rode of AHIMA's Washington office was instrumental in alerting me to resources and issues that helped shaped the advice and opinions offered in this book. Despite one of busiest health privacy-related schedules in the United States, Deven McGraw of the Center for Democracy and Technology took the time to offer an important perspective in the Foreword, and I am very grateful both for her generosity and her leadership on this issue. Thanks also go to the many AHIMA members whose questions and comments on the AHIMA communities of practice helped me better understand some of the most challenging aspects of implementing ARRA's provisions.

# Foreword

At the time of publication of *Privacy: The Impact of ARRA, HITECH, and Other Policy Initiatives,* we are on the cusp of what could be a watershed moment for the U.S. healthcare system. Congress is actively debating healthcare reform, focusing in particular on how individuals get access to health insurance, and national progress on this issue may be imminent. But the building blocks for health system reform were put in place earlier this year with the enactment of the American Recovery and Reinvestment Act of 2009 (ARRA)—in particular, the Health Information Technology for Economic and Clinical Health provisions. ARRA authorized what is now predicted to be a $46 billion federal investment to support the widespread adoption of health information technology (HIT)—electronic medical records and the electronic exchange of personal health information to improve healthcare and public health.

But the passage of ARRA also was a watershed moment for health privacy. Policymakers have long recognized (or at least paid lip service to) the importance of building public trust in health IT through the implementation of strong privacy and security provisions. However, previous health IT efforts were stymied in part by stark disagreements on how to address privacy. But for the first time in ARRA, Congress enacted significant health privacy provisions, amending a number of provisions in the Health Insurance Portability and Accountability Act (HIPAA) privacy and security regulations to address gaps in privacy protection that were raised or exacerbated by e-health initiatives. The ARRA privacy provisions are the most important development in health privacy since the implementation of the HIPAA rules.

Privacy advocates like me applauded the privacy provisions in ARRA. Industry stakeholders were, for the most part, relieved to break the "privacy log-jam"—but many also have raised concerns about how these new provisions will be implemented. I am not naïve about the enormous challenges we face in figuring out how to implement these provisions in a way that accomplishes their intent but also minimizes the burden on industry.

*Privacy: The Impact of ARRA, HITECH, and Other Policy Initiatives* will be an enormously valuable resource as we begin the long and challenging path to implementation. It provides a clear explanation of the changes in the law, identifies a number of issues that still needs to be resolved, and provides concrete suggestions for how organizations can be begin to come into compliance with the new legal requirements. We may not be finished shaping the details of ARRA's privacy provisions; however, the effective date for most of these provisions is only months away (and one particular provision—the obligation to notify patients in the event of a breach of their health data—is already in effect). Organizations must begin now to transition to the new world of health privacy, and this resource provides critical advice about how to get there.

What I appreciate most about *Privacy* is its tone, which acknowledges the critical importance of adequate safeguards for personal health information in building and maintaining public support for health IT while at the same time pointing out some of the more challenging aspects of particular ARRA provisions and providing practical advice about how to manage them. This is just what I would expect from Jill Dennis, the author of *Privacy*. I worked with Jill on the Privacy and Security Workgroup of the American Health Information Community and appreciate her passion for protecting privacy, which is matched by a common sense approach to developing and implementing privacy policy that stems from years of experience in the field. An appreciation of the importance of privacy as well as the difficulties associated with implementing new privacy protections is critical to developing workable and effective policy on this issue and is reflected throughout this book.

In these times of enormous change, uncertainty about the law hurts all of us, including consumers and patients. *Privacy* will help ensure that the privacy provisions enacted in ARRA are an enabler, and not an obstacle, to the widespread adoption and use of health IT to improve our healthcare system.

—Deven McGraw, JD, LLM, MPH

Washington, DC

# How to Use This Book

This book will be useful to a range of users—both those experienced with health information privacy issues and those just beginning to work with ARRA's HITECH provisions. After the overview and introduction to ARRA in chapter 1, chapter 2 describes the actual privacy provisions in detail. If you feel you already have a good understanding of what ARRA's HITECH provisions actually say, feel free to jump ahead to chapter 3, Operational Challenges, which delves deeper into what all this means from a practical perspective. However, if you haven't yet read the actual provisions in the law, I recommend that you first spend some time on chapters 1 and 2, which explain not only ARRA's goals and scope, but walk you through the most important provisions impacting privacy and security practices. (The law, in its entirety, is appendix C on the CD-ROM that accompanies this book.) Without that basic grounding in the rule, you'll be hard-pressed to understand the nuts-and-bolts operational challenges described, much less start planning for implementation. Over the course of many years spent educating others about HIPAA's Privacy Rule, I am still occasionally surprised by questions from privacy officers who have never taken the time to read the Rule itself. There's really no substitute for reading the actual language. And so, while I readily confess to not yet having tackled every one of the 407 pages of the entire Act yet, I've read Title XIII (the HITECH provisions that are the main focus of this book) more than a few times. If you have organizational responsibilities for privacy and/or security, you should too.

Once you're familiar with at least the key provisions of the law, start exploring the potential operational challenges these changes pose. Chapter 3 is devoted to exploring those issues, so that your organization can anticipate some likely problems and plan to avoid them.

Chapter 4 seeks to begin answering the questions, "what do I need to do?" and "when do I need to do it?" It is targeted at privacy and security officers, health information management directors, health informaticists, compliance officers, consultants and advisors, and the various others who assist in making things happen in organizations that create, collect, store, transmit, use, or disclose protected health information. As discussed, the list of organizations that qualify under that informal definition just got quite a bit longer. While there are technical aspects to some implementation strategies, the chapter focuses on administrative issues such as policy and procedural changes, training issues, contractual revisions, and the like.

Chapter 5 briefly discusses the interplay of ARRA with other privacy legislation, rules, and regulations. HIPAA's Privacy Rule is not the only game in town, and this chapter discusses the potential impact of ARRA on state laws, as well as other federal privacy mandates.

ARRA's language contains some ambiguities, and it uses many terms that have yet to be officially defined. As anyone in charge of regulatory compliance well understands, words matter. Chapter 6 summarizes ambiguities inherent in the legislation, some potential conflicts with existing laws and rules, and current plans for clarification, where they are known.

Chapter 7 is for those of you who wish to better understand the current U.S. health information privacy and security landscape. It covers the current efforts of many of the key players in privacy and security policy—some public and some private. Exploring this broader context can yield clues about future policy directions, unmet needs, and the issues most likely to catch fire in the near future.

A frequently-asked-questions (FAQs) format in appendix A delivers some of the same information as the chapters, but in a more targeted and specific way, when you are looking for a quick answer to a common question. Quick answers aren't always possible, but this appendix will help you when you need information on a very specific point.

The accompanying CD-ROM contains Web resources and links (appendix B) to help you gain access to the ever-expanding wealth of resources on ARRA, as well as more general health information privacy and security issues. It also contains a number of AHIMA practice tools on ARRA, and PDF versions of ARRA (appendix C), as well as the August 2009 regulations on breach notification from both the Department of Health and Human Services and from the Federal Trade Commission (appendixes D and E). The resources will be useful to those of you who need to know more than this book has the space to offer. The index will help you navigate quickly to the sections and topics you need the most.

It bears repeating: ARRA is new legislation—regulations to guide implementation and understanding its provisions are not yet all available. Those regulations, official advice, and future case law will flesh out a collective understanding of the "rules." This book provides an overview of where we are right now. Use it to help point you on the path to successful implementation of ARRA's changes and, ultimately, stronger privacy and security protections for health information.

# Chapter 1

# Overview of the American Recovery and Reinvestment Act of 2009's HITECH Provisions

Health information privacy is not a new concept. However, the healthcare industry's attention to privacy and security has grown substantially in recent years with the passage of the Health Insurance Portability and Accountability Act's (HIPAA) privacy and security regulations and now with the passage of the Health Information Technology for Economic and Clinical Health Act (HITECH) provisions of the American Reinvestment and Recovery Act of 2009 (ARRA). In many ways, this heightened legislative and regulatory attention reflects what is happening in American healthcare today: more and new kinds of organizations are involved in the care process—and these organizations have access to patients' health information.

## The Need for Legislation and Regulation

Most patients realize their information is available to their doctors and nurses and the various behind-the-scenes parties that work for a traditional hospital or physician's office. Fewer realize their information is often shared far more widely. Personal health information may be passing through health information exchanges, stored on various corporate servers, and accessible for purposes far beyond the provision of care. Policymakers' growing understanding of the complexity of $21^{st}$ century healthcare and public concerns over the potential implications of digital health information has gradually led to the establishment of baseline privacy protections and an expanding list of those obliged to safeguard patient information.

Congress had been active on health information privacy for a number of years. Many of the more recent bills were created out of concern for the growing use of computers in healthcare. Would it be easier to share electronic health information inappropriately? Could outside hackers break into healthcare organizations' medical records to steal patient information?

After a number of failed legislative attempts in the 1980s and 1990s, the provisions set forth from HIPAA opened the door for the Department of Health and Human Services (HHS) to issue health information privacy and security regulations in the event of Congressional inaction. The result was the Privacy Rule in 2000, which was amended in 2002, followed by the final security regulations in 2003.

Because those regulations required staff training in safeguarding patients' information, privacy and security became hot topics throughout the industry. All organizations covered by the new regulations (referred to as covered entities, defined under HIPAA as a provider, health plan, or clearinghouse) focused many hours on teaching their staff about privacy- and security-related matters, whether their patients' health information was held in paper, electronic, or hybrid formats. By many accounts, the privacy and security regulations were a true step forward in patient privacy protection.

Still, many commentators felt the HIPAA rules didn't go far enough. The rules only directly covered a subset of the parties actually holding, processing, and using health information. The rules did not take into account the development of new kinds of healthcare organizations that, although they do not provide care directly, do possess health information and therefore pose potential risks to patient privacy: entities such as health information exchanges and personal health record services run by commercial enterprises. Critics expressed concern that patients had no real protection against (or recourse in the event of) a privacy breach by one of these "noncovered entities" (referred to as *noncovered* since these organizations were not covered by HIPAA's Privacy Rule or security regulations).

These concerns seem well grounded in public opinion. A 2005 Harris Poll showed that overall, when told about electronic medical records, the public is equally split with 48 percent believing that the benefits outweigh the risks to privacy and 47 percent believing the risks outweigh the benefits (Westin 2005). During this same decade, the public saw frequent news reports of privacy breaches and misuses of health information.

At the same time, a growing number of private policy groups and professional associations were calling for enhanced health information privacy protections. The Markle Foundation's Connecting for Health initiative issued a number of papers calling for enhancements to HIPAA (Connecting for Health 2008a, 2–3) (Connecting for Health 2008b, 1–2). The American Health Information Management Association (AHIMA) issued a number of position statements and regulatory comment letters that called for expanded coverage of HIPAA, or HIPAA-like protections, so that health information would be protected no matter where it resides (AHIMA 2007, 2) (AMIA and AHIMA 2006, 2).

This combination of events, voices, and public pressures wasn't lost on the authors of the Privacy Rule and security regulations at the HHS. Having established an Office of the National Coordinator for Health Information Technology (ONC) in 2004 under the direction of David Brailer, MD, this office took on the task of exploring options for removing privacy concerns as a potential obstacle to the growing adoption of health information technology (HIT). There was, and still remains, a widely held belief in the power of HIT to improve care and reduce costs. But unless privacy and security concerns can be allayed and managed to the satisfaction of the American public, these concerns could derail our progress in the use of information technology to achieve gains in care and cost management.

To help guide the Secretary of HHS and the work of the ONC, the American Health Information Community (AHIC) was formed. It began its work in 2005, focusing on how best to achieve some key "breakthroughs" in care through the use of information technology. AHIC leadership quickly realized the need to focus on privacy and security issues associated with these breakthrough projects, and the Confidentiality, Privacy, and Security Workgroup of AHIC was formed later that year. Over the course of its existence, it issued a number of privacy-related recommendations to AHIC and the Secretary.

As the change in presidential administrations approached, work began to transition the AHIC, created by executive order, into more of a public–private partnership that could be sustained long-term. The result was the National eHealth Collaborative, which seeks to advance interoperability initiatives around health information technology.

During this same period, Congress was also interested in solidifying the gains in health IT adoption and promoting further advances through legislation. As Congress focused on economic recovery topics generally, the health IT adoption incentives and health information privacy protections of a currently pending bill (now referred to as the HITECH Act) were incorporated into a much larger bill focused on economic recovery: the ARRA. The Act passed both Houses of Congress and was signed by President Obama on February 17, 2009.

ARRA's HITECH provisions change HIPAA's privacy and security provisions in some fundamental and substantial ways, and with a number of implementing regulations scheduled within the Act itself, those changes will continue. A wide variety of organizations, both healthcare providers and many other healthcare-related organizations, need to be aware of these changes in order to successfully comply with the law and upcoming regulations. This book is about those changes, some of the key as-yet-unresolved questions about the law, and the operational challenges and potential impacts. Although the full impact of ARRA will not be settled for many years, this book suggests implementation strategies to minimize the risks of noncompliance during this transition to stronger health information privacy and security protections.

## ARRA

ARRA's primary focus is stimulating the U.S. economy through a variety of federal tax and spending provisions, including investing in a variety of essential public services in order to ensure the country's long-term economic health. Given the amount of healthcare spending in this country ($2.4 trillion in 2008) (Keehan et al. 2008), it's not surprising that a number of ARRA's provisions focus on the healthcare industry. Within Title XIII of ARRA, the Health Information

Technology for Economic and Clinical Health Act (HITECH) has several sections of particular interest for healthcare in the United States.

HITECH gives the Office of the National Coordinator for Health IT (ONC) statutory authorization to exist and has directed the ONC to create policy and standards' committees to promote health information technology (HIT) adoption through coordination of a national HIT policy and the promulgation of health IT standards.

HITECH also has directed the National Institute for Standards and Technology (NIST) to test the standards generated from the HIT standards committee and consult with the National Science Foundation to establish a program to assist in the development of Centers for Health Care Information Enterprise Integration. One of the purposes of these centers is to conduct research into HIT-related topics such as human-machine interfaces, voice recognition, improved interoperability, measuring the impact of IT on healthcare quality and productivity, and, notably, HIT security and integrity.

Grants and loan funding are also an important provision of the Act, directing the Secretary of HHS to invest funds through various federal agencies such as ONC, the Health Resources and Services Administration, the Agency for Healthcare Research and Quality (AHRQ), the Centers for Medicare and Medicaid Services (CMS), the Centers for Disease Control and Prevention (CDC), and the Indian Health Services (IHS), in order to support the development of a health IT architecture to support nationwide electronic health information exchange, promote the development and adoption of certified electronic health records (EHRs), and training on best practices for integrating HIT into care and delivery, among other purposes. The ONC was also directed to establish a health IT extension program (called Health IT Regional Extension Centers) to provide technology assistance to the healthcare industry and to add in applying research about best practices for HIT adoption, implementation, and use. State planning grants were made available to promote HIT adoption, as were the possibility of grants for demonstration projects to integrate HIT into clinical education programs. Of particular interest to the health information management (HIM) and informatics profession is Section 3016 of HITECH, which directs the Secretary to establish or expand medical health informatics education programs, including certification, undergraduate, and master's degree programs.

Outside of Title XIII, but of even greater interest to healthcare organization and providers, ARRA's Title IV, Section 4101 includes $17 billion in incentive payments (through the Medicare and Medicaid programs) to physicians and hospitals. In order to qualify for those incentive payments, a physician or hospital has to prove:

- The "meaningful" use of a certified EHR product with ePrescribing capability that meets HHS standards (what will constitute "meaningful" use is not yet settled, as is the question of who will be the source of "certification")

- Connectivity to other providers to enable electronic information exchange, in order to provide a full view of a patient's health history and status

- The ability to report the results of certain measures (not yet defined) to HHS using the technology

Incentive payments begin in 2011 and slowly ratchet down. That is the "carrot." There is also a "stick." For nonadopters, there will be penalties starting in 2015 for providers not engaging in "meaningful use" of electronic records.

For the purposes of this book, the real news of ARRA's HITECH is in Title XIII, Subtitle D–Privacy. This portion of the Act contains numerous changes to the privacy rules and security regulations of HIPAA. Why tinker with HIPAA? As mentioned earlier, HIPAA's Privacy Rule (and to perhaps a lesser extent, the security regulations) has long been criticized as failing to go far enough in protecting patient information. Although the rule mandated basic privacy protections, it did not apply to some of the new kinds of organizations that make up today's healthcare industry. For example, the Privacy Rule was not applicable to vendors of personal health record (PHR) systems, and with the growth of commercial PHR systems, many privacy advocates worry how individuals' health information will be protected from misuse (Center for Democracy and Technology 2008, 7). There have also been calls for privacy protection to "follow the data," rather than have health information protections be contingent on who happens to be holding the data (Patel and Rushefsky 2002, 189) (Nass et al. 2009, 258, 269).

Although ARRA doesn't go so far to extend privacy and security protection to all holders of protected health information nationwide, it does take a definite step beyond the limits of the Privacy Rule, as discussed in chapter 2. Further privacy enhancements can be expected in the form of various regulatory clarifications that ARRA requires the Secretary of HHS to issue. That schedule is discussed in chapter 3, Operational Challenges.

## Affected Parties

Although some sections of the Act have differing scopes of applicability, the overall list of those who are affected by ARRA is a long one. Specific applicability for each of the provisions is discussed in chapter 2. The kinds of parties taking notice of ARRA's changes to the HIPAA rules include:

- Covered entities (as defined by HIPAA rules) and the staff who work within them
- Business associates (also as defined by HIPAA rules) and the staff who work within them
- Vendors of PHRs (organizations that are not covered entities but offer or maintain a PHR) and their third-party service providers
- Electronic medical record and other health IT-related developers and vendors
- Marketing companies who work for healthcare clients
- Health information exchange organizations

- Researchers
- Law enforcement
- Media
- Regulators

ARRA's HITECH provisions very deliberately affect a larger universe than HIPAA did and will require companies previously untouched by federal privacy and security rules to come into compliance. For those readers who work for covered entities, or who are otherwise conversant with HIPAA's privacy and security provisions, you have a head start on compliance—even though ARRA's changes will be substantial. Those acquainting themselves with federal privacy and security regulations for the first time will need to become familiar with HIPAA's provisions as well as ARRA's HITECH amendments to HIPAA.

## The Big Picture

ARRA's main thrust is to strengthen the U.S. economy, and the bulk of the law consists of tax and spending provisions to accomplish that goal. However, no focus on the U.S. economy can ignore the impact of healthcare costs. By incorporating HITECH's provisions in ARRA, Congress clearly intends that the costs of healthcare be reduced, and the effectiveness increased, through the appropriate use of EHRs and other HIT.

The U.S. healthcare industry has been on an EHR implementation journey for many years, but the journey has been a long and difficult one for a variety of reasons. Some of those reasons are related to cost and uncertain return on investment (ROI) figures (RAND Corporation 2008), while others have to do with shortages of a skilled workforce to implement the changes that accompany new technology (AHIMA and AMIA 2006, 7). Another hindrance to EHR implementation is likely the difficulty in finding software that adapts well to existing workflows without extensive and expensive customization (American College of Physicians 2004, 4–5).

No less important than these issues is the public's concern and need for adequate safeguards for their personal health information. Individuals' acceptance of EHRs, electronic health information exchange, and even personal health record portals and health management tools will hinge on the confidence consumers have in the safety of their information. If they do not trust these systems, they will not use them and will seek opportunities to opt out where possible. Achieving large-scale benefits from HIT will require that the healthcare industry reach a critical mass in EHR use. So, the stakes are high for all of us. Health information privacy and security is a fundamental prerequisite to the widespread adoption of HIT. Each publicized mistake and news report of a breach hampers the industry's ability to achieve our goals. Whether one agrees with all of ARRA's HITECH provisions and the underlying HIPAA rules or not, compliance with these rules is one more step toward achieving the goals associated with HIT.

True compliance is not a one-time event. The journey doesn't end, and the target doesn't stop moving. ARRA was not the first step in health information privacy legislation, and it will not be the last. Various clarifying regulations will be issued with some frequency over the next several years. And with ARRA's statutory codification of the ONC, national attention to health information privacy and security will continue into the foreseeable future. Recognition of this long road ahead is not a reason for inaction or foot-dragging. There are things that can be done today to strengthen privacy- and security-related practices for the changes ARRA brings.

## **References**

AHIMA. 2007 (December). Statement on the Confidentiality, Privacy, and Security of Health Records. http://library.ahima.org/xpedio/groups/public/documents/ahima/bok1_036103.hcsp?dDocName=bok1_036103.

AHIMA, and AMIA. 2006. *Building the Workforce for Health Information Transformation.* www.amia.org/files/shared/Workforce_web.pdf.

American College of Physicians. Written Comments of the American College of Physicians on Incentives to Promote Health Information Technology, for the United States House of Representatives Committee on Ways and Means, Subcommittee on Health Hearing. June 17, 2004.

AMIA, and AHIMA. 2006 (July). *Statement on Health Information Confidentiality: A Joint Position Statement.* www.amia.org/files/amia_ahimajointconfidentialitystatement_0_.pdf.

American Recovery and Reinvestment Act (ARRA) of 2009. Public Law 111-5.

Center for Democracy and Technology. 2008 (May). *Comprehensive Privacy and Security: Critical for Health Information Technology, Version 1.0.* May 2008.

Connecting for Health. 2008a (February). *Policy Brief: Beyond Consumer Consent: Why We Need a Comprehensive Approach to Privacy in a Networked World.*

Connecting for Health. 2008b (September). *Policy Brief: We Need a 21st Century Approach to Allowing Americans to Protect and Share Health Information to Improve Quality.*

Keehan, S., et al. 2008. Health spending projections through 2017: The baby-boom generation is coming to Medicare. *Health Affairs* 27(2):w145-w155.

Nass, S. J., L. A. Levit, and Lawrence O. Gostin, eds. 2009. *Beyond the HIPAA Privacy Rule: Enhancing Privacy, Improving Health through Research.* Washington, DC: National Academies Press.

Patel, K., and M. E. 2002. Rushefsky. *Health Care Policy in an Age of New Technologies.* Armonk, NY: M. E. Sharpe.

RAND Corporation. 2009. RAND COMPARE: Overview of Health IT Policy Options. http://www.randcompare.org/options/mechanism/health_it.

Westin, A. F., and the Program on Health Information Technology, Health Records and Privacy. 2005. *How the Public Views Health Privacy: Survey Findings from 1978 to 2005.* Hackensack, NJ: CSLR.

# Chapter 2

# Key Provisions Impacting the HIPAA Privacy Rules

ARRA's scope is actually much broader than privacy and security. This chapter discusses the provisions that have implications for privacy and security practices and how those provisions affect the existing HIPAA Privacy Rules. A quick summary of these rules are listed in figure 2.1. This chapter examines, in detail, each of the issues listed.

**Figure 2.1.   Key highlights of ARRA related to healthcare privacy**

- The Office of the National Coordinator for Health Information Technology (ONC) is codified, and advisory committees for policy and standards established. The coordinator, along with the two committees, a to-be-named chief privacy officer, and existing HIPAA-related agencies will be addressing both the changes required by ARRA as well as other confidentiality, privacy, and security issues and standards identified as part of their process in the future.

- ARRA has several provisions that extend HIPAA privacy, security, and administrative requirements to business associations. In addition, there are new provisions for HIPAA-covered entities and business associates, as well as provisions for those not considered covered by HIPAA.

- Breach-related requirements (identification and notification) are established both for HIPAA-covered entities and noncovered entities, and implementing regulations were published in August 2009.

- The Act calls for HHS regional office privacy advisors and an education initiative on the uses of health information.

- Restrictions are further established on the sale of health information.

**Figure 2.1.   Key highlights of ARRA related to healthcare privacy** *(continued)*

- A new accounting requirement is established for disclosures related to treatment, payment, and healthcare operations—if those disclosures are through an EHR.

- New access rights are established for individuals related to obtaining healthcare information in electronic format.

- New conditions are instituted for the use of health information for marketing and fundraising functions.

- Personal health record (PHR) information with noncovered entities is now protected.

- Use of deidentified data, limited data sets, and the "minimum necessary" standard will be addressed in the future.

- Enforcement of the Privacy Rule is improved and penalties are increased.

- The HHS Secretary and the Federal Trade Commission (FTC) are required to provide a number of reports to Congress and guidance to the entities involved with healthcare data.

Source: Adapted from AHIMA. March 2009. *Analysis of Health Care Confidentiality, Privacy, and Security Provisions of the American Recovery and Reinvestment Act of 2009, Public Law 111-5,* 2.

## Codification of ONC and ONC Duties

The ONC was created by executive order of President George W. Bush. ARRA makes ONC a permanent part of the Department of Health and Human Services (HHS), and directs the ONC to accomplish a variety of privacy-related tasks, including:

- Updating the Federal Health IT Strategic Plan to include specific objectives, milestones, and metrics, such as:

  - "The incorporation of privacy and security protections for the electronic exchange of an individual's individually identifiable health information"

  - "Ensuring security methods to ensure appropriate authorization and electronic authentication of health information, and specifying technologies or methodologies for rendering health information unusable, unreadable, or indecipherable" (ARRA Section 3001)

- Appointing a chief privacy officer for ONC by February 17, 2010, whose duty will be to advise on privacy, security, and data stewardship of electronic health information and to coordinate with other federal agencies, with state and regional efforts, and with foreign countries with regard to the privacy, security, and data stewardship of electronic individually identifiable health information (ARRA Section 3001)

- Helping to establish two national advisory committees:
  - An HIT Policy Committee to make policy recommendations to ONC regarding implementation of a nationwide health IT infrastructure, including implementation of the strategic plan mentioned earlier (ARRA Section 3002)
  - An HIT Standards Committee to recommend to ONC standards, implementation specifications, and certification criteria for the electronic exchange and use of health information (ARRA Section 3003)

ARRA's codification of, and charges to, ONC ensure that the ONC will continue to play a key national role in driving national health information privacy and security policy, and will be a key source of guidance for those organizations seeking to implement ARRA's provisions. The ONC maintains a public Web site as part of the larger HHS health IT site. The health IT Web site (http://healthit.hhs.gov) (HHS 2009a) should be on the Favorites list of every privacy officer because it offers an excellent source for updates on federal privacy- and security-related activities, such as the committees previously noted.

## Key Business Associate Provisions

ARRA contains many changes for business associates of covered entities. Previously, business associates were not governed by HIPAA directly and were only obligated to follow the provisions in their business associate agreements with covered entities. This changes under ARRA, and most of the changes become effective on February 17, 2010. ARRA makes business associates independently subject to certain provisions of the HIPAA Privacy and Security rules, along with the civil and criminal penalties for violations. Business associates also will have to report security breaches to covered entities, subject to the breach notification requirements of Section 13402(b):

> A business associate of a covered entity that accesses, maintains, retains, modifies, records, stores, destroys, or otherwise holds, uses, or discloses unsecured protected health information shall, following the discovery of a breach of such information, notify the covered entity of such breach. Such notice shall include the identification of each individual whose unsecured protected health information has been, or is reasonably believed by the business associate to have been, accessed, acquired, or disclosed during such breach.

This notification must take place without unreasonable delay and in no case later than 60 calendar days after discovery of the breach. *Discovery* is considered to have occurred as of the first day on which the breach is actually known by the business associate (or its employees, officers, or agents), or should have reasonably been known. The burden of proof is on the business associate to demonstrate these notifications were made in a timely manner. If delays occur, they must be prepared to show evidence demonstrating the necessity of the delay.

It is important to note that the breach notification requirements only apply to "unsecured protected health information." That refers to PHI that is not secured through the use of a technology that makes the PHI unusable, unreadable, or indecipherable to unauthorized individuals (or other methodology approved by HHS, such as encryption of electronic data or destruction of paper). Therefore, if a memory stick containing encrypted PHI is lost or stolen, that would not trigger the breach notification requirements.

It is also important to note that the breach notification provisions are effective for breaches discovered on or after the date that is 30 days after the publication of final regulations on breach notification. Publication of the interim final rule on breach notification occurred in the August 24, 2009 *Federal Register,*(HHS 2009b), therefore making the effective date (both for business associates and for covered entities) September 23, 2009. However, HHS comments to these regulations indicate that sanctions will not be levied for six months after publication, due to the expected difficulties in implementing the necessary policy and procedural changes within a 30-day timeframe.

Business associates will also have to comply with the administrative, physical, and technical safeguards specified in HIPAA's security regulations, as well as the documentation requirements for policies and procedures outlined in the security regulations. Figures 2.2 through 2.6 outline the major requirements in these sections of the security regulations, and these figures are excerpted directly from the final security regulations of HIPAA. While reviewing them, notice that some of the implementation specifications (the subbullets) are required, while others are considered "addressable." Unless marked "addressable," the items described in each bullet and subbullet are required. For those marked "addressable," the business associate has some flexibility—it must assess whether the implementation specification is a reasonable and appropriate safeguard in its environment and, as applicable, either implement it or document why it would not be reasonable and appropriate, but also implement an equivalent alternative measure if reasonable and appropriate.

### Figure 2.2  Administrative safeguards now applicable to business associates

- **Security management process:** Implement policies and procedures to prevent, detect, contain, and correct security violations, through:
    - *Risk analysis*: An accurate and thorough assessment of the potential risks and vulnerabilities to the confidentiality, integrity, and availability of electronic protected health information (ePHI)
    - *Risk management*: Implement security measures sufficient to reduce risks and vulnerabilities to a reasonable and appropriate level.
    - *Sanction policy*: Apply appropriate sanctions against workforce members who fail to comply with security policies and procedures.
    - *Information system activity review*: Procedures to regularly review records of information system activity, such as audit logs, access reports, and security incident tracking reports.

- **Assigned security responsibility:** Identify the security official who is responsible for the development and implementation of these policies and procedures.

- **Workforce security:** Implement policies and procedures to ensure that all members of its workforce have appropriate access to ePHI under an information access management process, and to prevent those workforce members who do not have access under that process from obtaining access.

    - *Authorization and/or supervision*: Implement procedures for the authorization and/or supervision of workforce members who work with ePHI or in locations where it might be accessed (addressable requirement).

    - *Workforce clearance procedures*: Implement procedures to determine that the access of a workforce member to ePHI is appropriate (addressable).

    - *Termination procedures*: Implement procedures for terminating access to ePHI when the employment of a workforce member ends, or as required by determinations made under the clearance procedures noted above (addressable).

- **Information access management:** Implement policies and procedures for authorizing access to ePHI.

    - *Isolating healthcare clearinghouse functions*: If a healthcare clearinghouse is part of a larger organization, the clearinghouse must implement policies and procedures that protect the ePHI of the clearinghouse from the unauthorized access by the larger organization.

    - *Access authorization*: Implement policies and procedures for granting access to ePHI, for example, through access to a workstation, transaction, program, process, or other mechanism (addressable).

    - *Access establishment and modification*: Implement policies and procedures that, based upon the entity's access authorization policies, establish, document, review, and modify a user's right of access to a workstation, transaction, program, or process (addressable).

- **Security awareness and training:** Implement a security awareness and training program for all members of its workforce, including management.

    - *Security reminders*: Periodic security updates (addressable).

    - *Protection from malicious software*: Procedures for guarding against, detecting, and reporting malicious software (addressable).

    - *Log-in monitoring*: Procedures for monitoring log-in attempts and reporting discrepancies (addressable).

    - *Password management*: Procedures for creating, changing, and safeguarding passwords (addressable).

**Figure 2.2  Administrative safeguards now applicable to business associates** *(continued)*

- **Security incident procedures:** Implement policies and procedures to address security incidents.
  - *Response and reporting*: Identify and respond to suspected or known security incidents; mitigate, to the extent practicable, harmful effects of security incidents that are known; and document security incidents and their outcomes.
- **Contingency plan:** Establish (and implement as needed) policies and procedures for responding to an emergency or other occurrence (for example, fire, vandalism, system failure, and natural disaster) that damages systems that contain ePHI.
  - *Data back-up plan*: Establish and implement procedures to create and maintain retrievable exact copies of ePHI.
  - *Disaster recovery plan*: Establish (and implement as needed) procedures to restore any loss of data.
  - *Emergency mode operation plan*: Establish (and implement as needed) procedures to enable continuation of critical business processes for protection of the security of ePHI while operating in emergency mode.
  - *Testing and revision procedures*: Implement procedures for periodic testing and revision of contingency plans (addressable).
  - *Applications and data criticality analysis*: Assess the relative criticality of specific applications and data in support of other contingency plan components (addressable).
- **Business associate contracts required:** Written contract or other arrangement. Document the satisfactory assurances required in the security regulations' section on business associates (164.308(b)(1)) through a written contract or other arrangement that meets the applicable requirements of Section 164.314(a) (the security regulations' section on organizational requirements).

Source: 45 CFR 160, 162, and 164: Health insurance reform: Security standards. 2003.

**Figure 2.3  Physical safeguards now applicable to business associates**

- **Facility access controls:** Implement policies and procedures to limit physical access to its electronic information systems and the facility or facilities in which they are housed, while ensuring that properly authorized access is allowed.
- **Contingency operations:** Establish (and implement as needed) procedures that allow facility access in support of restoration of lost data under the disaster recovery plan and emergency mode operations plan in the event of an emergency (addressable).

# Key Provisions Impacting the HIPAA Privacy Rules

- ○ *Facility security plan*: Implement policies and procedures to safeguard the facility and the equipment therein from unauthorized physical access, tampering, and theft (addressable).

- ○ *Access control and validation procedures*: Implement procedures to control and validate a person's access to facilities based on their role or function, including visitor control, and control of access to software programs for testing and revision (addressable).

- ○ *Maintenance records*: Implement policies and procedures to document repairs and modifications to the physical components of a facility which are related to security (for example, hardware, walls, doors, and locks) (addressable).

- **Workstation use:** Implement policies and procedures that specify the proper functions to be performed, the manner in which those functions are to be performed, and the physical attributes of the surroundings of a specific workstation or class of workstation that can access ePHI.

- **Workstation security:** Implement physical safeguards for all workstations that access ePHI, to restrict access to authorized users.

- **Device and media controls:** Implement policies and procedures that govern the receipt and removal of hardware and electronic media that contain ePHI into and out of a facility, and the movement of these items within the facility.

  - ○ *Disposal*: Implement policies and procedures to address the final disposition of ePHI, and/or the hardware or electronic media on which it is stored.

  - ○ *Media re-use*: Implement procedures for removal of ePHI from electronic media before the media are made available for reuse.

  - ○ *Accountability*: Maintain a record of the movements of hardware and electronic media and any person responsible therefore (addressable).

  - ○ *Data backup and storage*: Create a retrievable, exact copy of ePHI, when needed, before movement of equipment (addressable).

Source: 45 CFR 160, 162, and 164: Health insurance reform: Security standards. 2003.

## Figure 2.4  Technical safeguards now applicable to business associates

- **Access control:** Implement technical policies and procedures for electronic information systems that maintain ePHI to allow access only to those persons or software programs that have been granted access rights.

  - ○ *Unique user identification*: Assign a unique name and/or number for identifying and tracking user identity.

  - ○ *Emergency access procedure*: Establish (and implement as needed) procedures for obtaining necessary ePHI during an emergency.

- *Automatic log-off*: Implement electronic procedures that terminate an electronic session after a predetermined time of inactivity (addressable).

- *Encryption and decryption*: Implement a mechanism to encrypt and decrypt ePHI (addressable).

- **Integrity:** Implement policies and procedures to protect ePHI from improper alteration or destruction.

  - *Mechanism to authenticate ePHI*: Implement electronic mechanisms to corroborate that ePHI has not been altered or destroyed in an unauthorized manner (addressable).

- **Person or entity authentication**: Implement procedures to verify that a person or entity seeking access to ePHI is the one claimed.

- **Transmission security**: Implement technical security measures to guard against unauthorized access to ePHI that is being transmitted over an electronic communications network.

  - *Integrity controls*: Implement security measures to ensure that electronically transmitted ePHI is not improperly modified without detection until disposed of (addressable).

  - *Encryption*: Implement a mechanism to encrypt ePHI whenever deemed appropriate (addressable).

Source: 45 CFR 160, 162, and 164: Health insurance reform: Security standards. 2003.

**Figure 2.5 Policies and procedures documentation requirements now applicable to business associates**

- **Policies and procedures:** Implement reasonable and appropriate policies and procedures to comply with the standards, implementation specifications, or other requirements of the HIPAA security regulations (sections specified in the rule).

- **Documentation:** Maintain the policies and procedures implemented to comply with the security regulations in written (which may be electronic) form; and if an action, activity, or assessment required by the regulations is required to be documented, maintain a written record of it.

  - *Time limit*: Retain the documentation for 6 years from the date of its creation or the date when it was last in effect, whichever is later.

  - *Availability*: Make documentation available to those persons responsible for implementing the procedures to which the documentation pertains.

  - *Updates*: Review documentation periodically, and update as needed, in response to environmental or operational changes affecting the security of the ePHI.

Source: 45 CFR 160, 162, and 164: Health insurance reform: Security standards. 2003.

## Key Provisions Impacting the HIPAA Privacy Rules

Because so many of these requirements are new to business associates, all business associates will need to increase their privacy and security compliance efforts. New policies and procedures will need to be written, and new kinds of staff training will be needed. In addition, existing business associate agreements will need to be rewritten to reflect the new requirements.

ARRA also adds a new prohibition on business associates (as well as covered entities) selling any individual's protected health information without the specific authorization of the individual (ARRA Section 13405(d)). That authorization must also specify whether the entity receiving the PHI can further exchange that information for remuneration. There are some exceptions, for example, public health and research data, as defined by HIPAA, when the purpose of the exchange is for treatment (subject to any regulation the Secretary may promulgate), when the purpose of the exchange is for healthcare operations (activities related to the business management and general administrative activities of the entity, including certain sales, transfers, mergers, or consolidations), when the purpose is for remuneration that is provided by a covered entity to a business associate for activities involving the exchange of PHI that the business associate undertakes on behalf of and at the specific request of the covered entity pursuant to a business associate agreement, when the purpose is to provide an individual with a copy of their own PHI pursuant to HIPAA's "access" provisions, and when the purposes of the exchange is otherwise determined by the Secretary in regulations to be necessary and appropriate. The Secretary will be issuing regulations on the issue of selling PHI, but at press time those regulations have not yet been issued.

Another ARRA issue impacting business associates is the accounting of disclosures. Under HIPAA's Privacy Rule, covered entities were required to maintain an accounting, but business associates were not (unless, of course, they were contractually obliged to do so under their business associate agreement). ARRA's Section 13405(c) directs covered entities to either choose to account for their business associates' disclosures or provide a list of all business associates to an individual so that individual can directly request an accounting from the business associate. The business associate, in turn, must then provide the accounting of disclosures made by that business associate.

This option only applies to the new accounting requirements associated with disclosures if the covered entity uses an electronic record. The Secretary will issue regulations on what information must be collected about each such disclosure not later than six months after the date on which the Secretary adopts standards for the accounting of disclosures. The effective date of this new provision is triggered by whether and when the covered entity begins using an electronic record. For electronic records in place as of January 1, 2009, the accounting requirement will apply to disclosures on and after January 1, 2014. For subsequent adopters of electronic records, the provisions will apply to disclosures made on or after the later of the following: January 1, 2011, or the date that it acquires an EHR. The Secretary is free to set a later date, if the Secretary determines that it is necessary, but in no case may that date be later than 2013 for adopters after January 1, 2009, or later than 2016 for adopters prior to January 1, 2009.

This new requirement is likely to be problematic for business associates in a number of ways. First, most are not familiar with the accounting of disclosures requirement, and our experience with the implementation process in covered entities teaches us that there will be a good deal of confusion and expense associated with implementation. In addition, it is very conceivable that a business associate may have some covered entity clients who want to do the accounting themselves and other clients who push that responsibility onto the business associate. Having a way of separating which disclosures must be accounted for, based on the covered entity's preferences, will be important. Even more difficult is the fact that this requirement only applies to disclosures when the covered entity (client) has an electronic record, perhaps again requiring a sorting process to establish accounting procedures for only those clients. The fact that the effective dates will vary, based on when the covered entity client implemented that electronic record, is yet another complication. One can envision situations in which the covered entity client makes disclosures through an electronic record, triggering the obligation to account, but the business associate may not have electronic capabilities—thus requiring the manual tracking of all eligible disclosures by the business associate. Business associates will want to begin considering these possibilities now, and watch closely for clarifying regulations.

Similarly, the provisions that give patients the right to access their PHI in an electronic format appear to also affect business associates who maintain that information on behalf of a covered entity. ARRA's Section 13404 allows business associates to use and disclose PHI only if they are in compliance with each applicable requirement of Section 164.504(3) of the HIPAA Privacy Rule—the business associate contracts section. And that section requires the contract to provide that the business associate will make PHI available to the patient in line with Section 164.524 of the Privacy Rule (where access to individuals, and format of such access, are discussed).

These changes have teeth. Under ARRA, business associates can be held directly accountable for failure to comply with any HIPAA Privacy Rule provisions made applicable through their contracts with covered entities. And, because these contracts (business associate agreements) will need to specifically incorporate the new obligations of business associates, the expansion of potential liability is clear. As of February 17, 2009, most of the civil and criminal penalties of HIPAA noncompliance are as applicable to business associates as they are to covered entities. (Further guidance is expected to be issued for certain enforcement requirements.)

ARRA has expanded the existing civil penalties and enforcement provisions and categorized them into "tiers," as described in figure 2.6.

### Figure 2.6  Civil penalties for ARRA violations

- **Tier 1:** When the person is unaware of the violation, and would not have known even with reasonable diligence, the penalty is at least $100 per violation not to exceed $25,000 for all violations of the same requirement during the year.

- **Tier 2:** When the violation is due to reasonable cause and not willful neglect, the penalty is at least $1,000 per violation not to exceed $100,000 for all violations of the same requirement during the year.

- **Tier 3:** When the violation is due to willful neglect (which is expected to be defined by the Secretary in August 2010) but is corrected within 30 days, the penalty is at least $50,000 per violation, not to exceed $250,000 for all violations of the same requirement during the year.

- **Tier 4:** When the violation is due to willful neglect and is not corrected within 30 days, the penalty is at least $50,000 per violation not to exceed $1,500,000 for all violations of the same requirement during the year.

ARRA also expands enforcement provisions by providing state attorneys general with the authority to bring civil actions in federal courts against any person whose violations pose a threat to, or harms, one or more residents of that state. Actions can be brought to enjoin violations or seek damages. In addition, the HHS Secretary will now be required to conduct periodic compliance audits of covered entities and business associates. There are provisions for mandatory formal investigation by the Secretary of complaints, and penalties must be imposed where violations are determined to be due to willful neglect. This is a more aggressive approach to enforcement than the industry saw under HIPAA.

In addition to extending civil and criminal liability under HIPAA to business associates, ARRA indicates that criminal penalties may also apply to an individual or employee that obtains or discloses PHI without authorization, as long as that information is maintained by a covered entity.

Under the HIPAA Privacy Rule, covered entities were required to take action if they were aware of a business associate's noncompliance with the agreement. Under ARRA, the need to take action becomes a two-way street (ARRA Section 13404(b)). A business associate who becomes aware of a pattern of activity or practice of the covered entity that constitutes a material breach or violation of their obligations must, unless reasonable and successful steps are taken to cure the breach or end the violation, terminate the agreement, or if that is not feasible, report the problem to the Secretary. Business associates who fail to do this can be subject to the Act's penalties.

## Breach Notification Provisions

Breach notification is one of the provisions of ARRA that will require substantial changes in covered entities' privacy-related policies and procedures. Clearly, affected organizations will need to have systems in place not only to prevent and detect breaches, but to notify patients promptly. What was previously an often slow, deliberative, "one-off" decision-making process under HIPAA that weighed the benefits of risk mitigation through notification against the risks of undue alarm and disruption of the patient–provider relationship and public relations fallout, will now need to become a quicker, more consistent business routine that is well understood and well executed by staff.

Before examining the notification requirements, it's important to understand the definition of *breach*, first as defined in Section 13400 of ARRA, and as slightly restated in the HHS breach notification regulations issued August 24, 2009. In ARRA, *breach* means the unauthorized acquisition, access, use, or disclosure of PHI, which compromises the security or privacy of such information, except where an unauthorized person to whom such information is disclosed would not reasonably have been able to retain such information. The term does not include any unintentional acquisition, access, or use of PHI by an employee or individual acting under the authority of a covered entity or business associate, if such acquisition, access, or use was made in good faith and within the course and scope of the employment or other professional relationship of that individual and the information is not further acquired, accessed, used, or disclosed without authorization by any person.

The August 24, 2009 HHS breach notification regulations restate the definition of *breach* to mean the acquisition, access, use, or disclosure of protected health information in a manner not permitted under subpart E of this part (meaning the Privacy Rule), which compromises the security or privacy of the protected health information (45 CFR 164.402). The phrase "compromises the security or privacy of the PHI" means "poses a significant risk of financial, reputational, or other harm to the individual." A use or disclosure of PHI that does not include the identifiers listed in section 164.514(e)(2), date of birth, and zip code (basically, the limited data set elements plus date of birth and zip code) does *not*, according to HHS, compromise the security or privacy of the PHI (but note that HHS has sought public comments on this issue, and this qualifier could change in the future).

As in the original definition under ARRA, there are some exceptions to the definition of breach. The definition excludes:

- Any unintentional acquisition, access, or use of PHI by a workforce member or person acting under the authority of a covered entity or a business associate, if such acquisition, access, or use was made in good faith and within the scope of authority and does not result in further use or disclosure in a manner not permitted by the Privacy Rule

- Any inadvertent disclosure by a person who is authorized to access PHI at a covered entity or business associate to another person authorized to access PHI at the same covered entity, business associate, or organized health care arrangement in which the covered entity participates, and the information received as a result of such disclosure is not further used or disclosed in a manner not permitted under the Privacy Rule

- A disclosure of PHI where a covered entity or business associate has a good faith belief that an unauthorized person to whom the disclosure was made would not reasonably have been able to retain such information (45 CFR 164.402(2)).

This definition raises several interesting issues. First, this definition may be at odds with some of the breach definitions found in state laws or regulations. Covered entities and business associates will need to exercise care in writing their policies governing breach response and notification to ensure that all applicable legal requirements are met. Second, under what circumstances would the unauthorized person receiving PHI not reasonably be able to retain the information? (HHS comments to the August 2009 regulations use two examples: (1) "explanations of benefits" letters that were sent to the wrong individuals, but returned, unopened, as undeliverable, from the post office; and (2) a nurse hands the wrong patient's discharge papers to the patient, but realizes the mistake and takes it back before the patient reads it.) Third, if relying on the second bulleted exception to breach listed earlier, how will the original disclosing party even know if the recipient further uses or discloses the PHI in a manner not permitted by the Privacy Rule? These exceptions will likely be a source of some ongoing confusion and debate.

ARRA requires that breaches be treated as discovered by the covered entity or business associate on the first day on which the breach is either actually known to the organization (to any person in the organization, other than the individual committing the breach, such as other employees, officers, or other agents), or the first day on which the breach should reasonably have been known to the organization. This section of ARRA was also changed slightly by the August 24, 2009 regulations, by changing the language referring to employees or officers to refer to "workforce" members, as defined in the Privacy Rule. Breaches are to be treated as discovered by a covered entity as of the first day on which such breach is known to the covered entity or, by exercising reasonable diligence, would have been known to the covered entity. And a covered entity shall be deemed to have knowledge or a breach if such breach is known, or by exercising reasonable diligence would have been known, to any person, other than the person committing the breach, who is a workforce member or agent of the covered entity (determined in accordance with the federal common law of agency). Organizations without timely methods of detecting, responding to, and reporting breaches will likely face challenges by regulators and plaintiffs as to whether they should have known earlier.

Once a breach occurs, covered entities must notify the individual(s) whose unsecured PHI has been, or is reasonably believed by the covered entity to have been, accessed, acquired, used, or disclosed as a result of such breach (45 CFR 164.404(a)(1)). Notifications must be made without unreasonable delay and in no case later than 60 calendar days after the discovery of the breach. The burden for demonstrating that notifications were made as required, including demonstrating proof of the necessity of any delay, belongs to the covered entity or business associate (ARRA Section 13402(d)(1)).

Notices to individuals whose PHI has been breached must be provided in writing by first-class mail to the individual or next of kin at the last known address or, if specified by the individual, by electronic mail. In cases where urgency is required because of possible imminent misuse of unsecured PHI, additional notice can occur by telephone or other means—but this supplements, rather than takes the place of, the requirement for written notice by first-class mail (ARRA

Section 13402(e)(1)(A) and (C)). If there is insufficient or outdated contact information that precludes direct written (or electronic, if specified by the individual) notice, a substitute form of notice is required. If there are 10 or more individuals for which there is insufficient or outdated contact information, a conspicuous posting on the covered entity's Web site, or notice given in major print or broadcast media in geographic areas where the individuals affected by the breach are likely to reside. In the case of a Web site posting, the Secretary will determine the required period of posting. Although the law does not absolutely require it, ARRA indicates that media or Web postings "will likely include a toll-free number where an individual can learn whether or not the individual's unsecured protected health information is possibly included in the breach" (ARRA Section 13402(e)(1)(b)).

In larger scale breaches (actual or reasonably believed to have occurred) involving the unsecured PHI of more than 500 residents of a given state or jurisdiction, notice must be provided to prominent media outlets serving that state or jurisdiction (ARRA Section 13402(e)(2)).

Notice must also be provided to the Secretary (by covered entities) of unsecured PHI that has been acquired or disclosed in a breach. If that breach involves less than 500 individuals, the covered entity may maintain a log of any such breach occurring and annually submit that log to the Secretary, documenting such breaches occurring during the year involved. On the other hand, if the breach involves 500 or more individuals, the notice to the Secretary must occur contemporaneously with the required notification of the patient (45 CFR 164.408(b)). The Secretary must make available on the public HHS Web site a list of each covered entity involved in a breach that involved the unsecured PHI of more than 500 individuals (ARRA Section 13402(e)(4)).

Both ARRA and the August breach notification regulations speak to the required content of breach notifications to individuals. The following items should be included, to the extent possible (ARRA Section 13402(f) and 45 CFR 164.404(a)(2)(c)):

- A brief description of what happened, including the date of the breach and date of discovery, if known

- A description of the types of unsecured PHI that were involved in the breach (such as full name, social security number, date of birth, home address, account number, diagnosis, disability code, or other types of information)

- The steps individuals should take to protect themselves from potential harm resulting from the breach

- A brief description of what the covered entity involved is doing to investigate the breach, to mitigate harm to the individuals, and to protect against any further breaches

- Contact procedures for individuals to ask questions or learn additional information, which shall include a toll-free telephone number, an e-mail address, Web site, or postal address

## Key Provisions Impacting the HIPAA Privacy Rules

In situations where a law enforcement official determines that a required notification, notice, or posting would impede a criminal investigation or cause damage to national security, Section 13402(g) of ARRA requires the delay of that notice/posting, in the same manner as accomplished in HIPAA's Privacy Rule Section 164.528(a)(2). This HIPAA provision requires the law enforcement official to provide a written statement to the effect that the notice/posting would be likely to impede an investigation, and it must specify a time limit for the suspension of notification. Alternatively, if these assurances are made orally by a law enforcement official, the covered entity must document the statement, including the identity of the agency or official making the statement, temporarily suspend the notice/posting, and limit that suspension to no longer than 30 days from the date of the oral statement, unless a written statement is offered during that time.

ARRA also requires the Secretary to periodically report information about breaches to key Congressional Committees. The reports are to include the number and nature of the breaches reported and the actions taken in response (ARRA Section 13402(i)).

There are also some temporary breach notification requirements in ARRA for vendors of PHRs and other noncovered entities. These requirements are found in Section 13407 and apply not only to vendors of PHRs but also to entities:

- Offering products or services through the Web site of a vendor of PHRs

- Other than covered entities, that offer products or services through the Web sites of covered entities that offer individuals PHRs

- Other than covered entities, that access information in a PHR or send information to a PHR.

These provisions of ARRA were followed by the August 25, 2009 *Federal Register* publication of a final rule on Health Breach Notification by the FTC.

Following the discovery of a breach of information, the entity must notify each individual who is a citizen or resident of the United States whose unsecured PHR identifiable health information was acquired by an authorized person as a result of breach of security. They must also notify the FTC.

Third-party service providers to vendors of PHRs or the entities listed earlier must also report breaches of security to the vendor or applicable entity. That notice must include the identification of each individual whose unsecured PHR identifiable health information has been, or is reasonably believed to have been, accessed, acquired, or disclosed during the breach (ARRA Section 13407(b)). These noncovered entity vendors must follow ARRA's breach notification requirements in a manner to be specified by the FTC, and the FTC will notify the HHS Secretary.

Violations of ARRA by these noncovered entities will be treated as unfair and deceptive acts or practices in violation of regulations promulgated under the Federal Trade Commission Act.

Notably, what constitutes a "breach of security" for these kinds of noncovered entities has been specifically listed in ARRA Section 13407(f). A breach of security means, with respect to unsecured PHR identifiable health information of an individual in a personal health record, "acquisition of such information without the authorization of the individual." This is not the same as the breach definition governing covered entities and business associates; this definition is not qualified with exceptions.

"PHR identifiable health information" has also been defined in Section 13407(f). It means individually identifiable health information as defined by HIPAA that is provided by or on behalf of the individual *and* identifies the individual (or for which there is a reasonable basis to believe that the information can be used to identify the individual).

This section of ARRA will require privacy compliance by a new class of entities that are not covered entities under HIPAA. As noted earlier, the FTC issued final regulations for this section on August 25, 2009. The provisions of this section will apply to breaches of security discovered on or after September 24, 2009. However, if Congress enacts new legislation establishing requirements for breach of security notifications by noncovered entities or entities that are not business associates, this section will sunset once those new regulations go into effect.

## Requests for Restrictions on Certain Disclosures

Under the HIPAA Privacy Rule, individuals were able to request restrictions on disclosures, but the covered entity did not have to agree to honor those requests. ARRA gives patients more power in obtaining desired restrictions on disclosures of their health information. However, under Section 13405 of ARRA, covered entities *must* comply with a requested restriction if the disclosure is to a health plan for the purposes of payment or healthcare operations (not for treatment), under certain limited circumstances. This change will require some careful parsing of information when restriction requests are received and as requests for release of information are received from health plans. In the past, many facilities made it an unwritten rule to decline all restriction requests simply because of the administrative difficulty of honoring such requests. As a result, restriction-related policies and procedures will need to be reworked and staff will require education.

Under Section 13405 of ARRA, covered entities must comply with the requested restriction under these circumstances (ARRA Section 13405(a)(1)(2)):

- Except as otherwise required by law, if the disclosure is to a health plan for the purpose of carrying out payment or health care operations (and is not for purposes of treatment); and
- The PHI pertains solely to a health care item of service for which the health care provider involved has been paid out of pocket in full

This provision will permit patients to avoid sharing health information with their insurer, if they choose to pay directly (and fully) for the care out of pocket. Covered entities will need to establish new procedures for segregating, for the purposes of disclosures to health plans for non-treatment uses, the information pertaining to care paid for by the patient versus that paid for by the plan. Although it may sound straightforward on its face, the practical reality is that this restriction could apply to an entire encounter, or just a single test among many, so the process will need to take this granularity into account. And it won't be as simple as having special procedures for all health plan disclosures, since this provision makes an exception for treatment-related disclosures (for example, such as when a health insurer is providing chronic condition care management for one of their insureds).

## Restrictions on the Sale of Health Information

Section 13405(d) of ARRA prohibits the sale of PHI by covered entities (and business associates, as noted earlier in this chapter) unless permitted by a valid authorization. It includes both direct and indirect remuneration, and the meanings of these will require further clarification in regulations. That authorization must also specify whether the entity receiving the PHI can further exchange that information for remuneration.

There are some exceptions—for example, public health and research data, as defined by HIPAA, when the purpose of the exchange is for treatment (subject to any regulation the Secretary may promulgate), when the purpose of the exchange is for healthcare operations (activities related to the business management and general administrative activities of the entity, including certain sales, transfers, mergers, or consolidations), when the purpose is for remuneration that is provided by a covered entity to a business associate for activities involving the exchange of PHI that the business associate undertakes on behalf of and at the specific request of the covered entity pursuant to a business associate agreement, when the purpose is to provide an individual with a copy of their own PHI pursuant to HIPAA's "access" provisions, and when the purpose of the exchange is otherwise determined by the Secretary in regulations to be necessary and appropriate. The Secretary must issue regulations on this issue of selling PHI by August 17, 2010. Once issued, the rule will apply to exchanges occurring on or after February 17, 2011.

## Right to Access in Electronic Form

ARRA also requires covered entities using or maintaining EHRs to provide requesting individuals with an electronic copy of their protected health information. The individual may also direct the covered entity to transmit a copy directly to entities or persons of that individual's choosing. Fees for providing such electronic copies (or electronic summaries or explanations of that information) cannot exceed the covered entity's actual labor costs in responding to the request. Under HIPAA, patients could request that their health information be provided in electronic format, but the covered entity was not required to provide the data in electronic format if it was not "readily reproducible" in that format (ARRA Section 164.524(c)(2)). It was up to the covered entity to decide whether the data was "readily reproducible." Although it's now commonplace for imaging providers to give patients DVDs containing their imaging studies, electronic medical record (EMR) software does not always offer users a simple method of moving selected health information onto a DVD, CD, or other electronic form. Often it can be done, but not without considerable effort. The "readily reproducible" loophole disappears in ARRA, and as a result EMR software vendors will need to ensure their software includes this functionality.

This provision of ARRA will require covered entities to fully understand their labor costs associated with responding to these requests. What may be a simple process with one vendor's software may be far more difficult in another covered entity. In addition, a number of states have statutes or regulations defining standard fees for responding to these types of requests, and those formulae may well conflict with this requirement. As a result, covered entities may have more than one fee schedule, depending on the nature of the request.

## Accounting of Disclosures

Changes have also affected HIPAA's requirements for an accounting of disclosures. Perhaps no Privacy Rule provision has been more frustrating for health information management (HIM) departments, due to the need to spend both time and money implementing a process for the accounting in spite of the fact that patients very rarely request such an accounting. In addition, when patients do request an accounting, often they find the accounting doesn't document the kinds of things in which patients are most interested, for example, internal accesses, healthcare operations uses and disclosures, and such.

ARRA changes the Privacy Rule's approach to accounting in an interesting way: if a covered entity (or business associate, in cases where covered entities have delegated accounting duties for business associate disclosures) uses or maintains an electronic health record, the HIPAA exception for tracking and documenting disclosures for treatment, payment, and healthcare operations no longer applies if that disclosure is made "through an electronic health record." (ARRA Section 13405(c)(1)(A)). In addition, in this situation, individuals have the right to receive an accounting of disclosures made by the covered entity during the three years prior to the date on which the accounting is requested.

The Secretary will issue regulations on what information must be collected about each such disclosure not later than six months after the date on which the Secretary adopts standards for the accounting of disclosures. The effective date of this new provision is triggered by whether and when the covered entity begins using an electronic record. For electronic records in place as of January 1, 2009, the accounting requirement will apply to disclosures on and after January 1, 2014. For subsequent adopters of electronic records, the provisions will apply to disclosures made on or after the later of the following: January 1, 2011, or the date that it acquires an EHR. The Secretary is free to set a later date, if the Secretary determines that it is necessary, but in no case may that date be later than 2013 for adopters after January 1, 2009, or later than 2016 for adopters prior to January 1, 2009.

While this change will eventually make the accounting more meaningful for individuals who want to see how their health information has been disclosed, it will complicate the accounting process considerably and is bound to be the source of much confusion. Just because a covered entity uses an electronic record, it does not follow that treatment, payment, and healthcare operations-related disclosures are made "through" the software and are therefore tracked within that software. Release of information may still be done manually or use stand-alone software applications that cannot lift and transmit data directly out of EHR software. Therefore, this provision will require accounting for an expanded number of disclosures, but it will not capture the entire universe of treatment, payment, and healthcare operations disclosures. It will likely add a good deal of administrative burden to covered entities, without compensation. Some commentators believe that tracking treatment, payment, and healthcare operations-related disclosures will be "simple" (Gellman 2009, 10). In reality, it is not likely to be quite so simple, and chapters 3 and 4 explore the potential difficulties as well as possible strategies to assist in implementing this provision.

As noted earlier, there are also new provisions permitting covered entities to refer individuals to their business associates to obtain an accounting of the business associate's disclosures that are covered by the accounting rules. The option of doing this belongs to the covered entity—it may choose to continue accounting for these disclosures itself or provide requesting individuals with a list of its business associates. See the Key Business Associate Provisions section of this chapter for more specifics.

## Minimum Necessary and the Limited Data Set

Changes are also coming to HIPAA's "minimum necessary" provisions. Section 13405(b)(1) of ARRA requires covered entities to limit most uses, disclosures, and requests of protected health information to the HIPAA-defined "limited data set," to the extent practicable. Below are the data elements in the limited data set. If more information is needed, the "minimum necessary" information to accomplish the intended purpose should be used. But this alternative appears only to apply if the limited data set will not serve the purpose.

### Limited Data Set (HIPAA Privacy Rule, Section 164.512(e)(2))

A *limited data set* is protected health information that excludes the following direct identifiers of the individual or of relatives, employers, or household members of the individual:

- Names
- Postal address information, other than town or city, state, and zip code
- Telephone numbers
- Fax numbers

- E-mail addresses
- Social security numbers
- Medical record numbers
- Health plan beneficiary numbers
- Account numbers
- Certificate/license numbers
- Vehicle identifiers and serial numbers, including license plate numbers
- Device identifiers and serial numbers
- Web universal resource locators (URLs)
- Internet protocol (IP) address numbers
- Biometric identifiers, including finger and voice prints
- Full face photographic images and any comparable images

As was true under HIPAA, the disclosing entity—at least at this time—determines what constitutes the "minimum necessary." But ARRA Section 164.512(e)(2) requires the HHS Secretary to issue guidance on what constitutes the "minimum necessary" by August 17, 2010. Once that guidance is effective, this provision of ARRA will expire. Therefore, in essence, ARRA includes some interim requirements for covered entities to use the limited data set, where practicable, until the Secretary-issued guidance on minimum necessary is effective. In this interim period, the language appears to heighten the obligation of covered entities to more carefully limit uses and disclosures, with the continuing exceptions of treatment-related disclosures, disclosures to the individual, disclosures pursuant to a valid authorization, disclosures to the Secretary, and uses and disclosures required by law or required for compliance with HIPAA.

The need for limiting disclosures to items contained in the limited data set, or in the alternative, the need to make a determination as to minimum necessary, does not apply to deidentified PHI.

It's obvious from the preceding list that a limited data set is a subset of PHI that is stripped of many identifiers. It has had fairly limited use since the Privacy Rule's enactment for just that reason: it often doesn't fully accomplish the purpose of the disclosure. Even so, under ARRA covered entities will have to first consider whether the limited data set would meet the purposes of the requests they receive.

## New Conditions for Marketing and Fundraising Contacts

Section 13406 of ARRA makes a number of changes to the Privacy Rule's treatment of the use of PHI for marketing and fundraising contacts. This portion of the Privacy Rule had been the source of some confusion as to whether a particular communication was "marketing" versus a "healthcare operation." If one could classify the communication as a healthcare operation, no individual authorization was required. However, covered entities could not use PHI for "marketing" communications without valid authorization from the individual (again, with some exceptions).

ARRA clarifies that "a communication by a covered entity or business associate that is about a product or service and that encourages recipients of the communication to purchase or use the product or service shall not be considered a healthcare operation" unless the communication is:

- To describe a health-related product or service (or payment for such product or service) that is provided by, or included in a plan of benefits of, the covered entity making the communication, including communications about:
  - Entities participating in a healthcare provider network or health plan network
  - Replacement of, or enhancements to, a health plan
  - Health-related products or services available only to a health plan enrollee that add value to, but are not part of, a plan of benefits
- For treatment of the individual
- For case management or care coordination for the individual, or to direct or recommend alternative treatments, therapies, healthcare providers, or settings of care to the individual

In addition, even a communication covered by one of these bulleted exceptions will not be considered healthcare operations if the covered entity receives or has received direct or indirect payment (does not include payment for treatment) in exchange for making such communications, except where:

- The communication describes only a drug or biologic that is currently being prescribed for the recipient of the communication and any payment received by the covered entity in exchange for making this communication is "reasonable" in amount
- Each of the following conditions apply:
  - The communication is made by the covered entity
  - The covered entity making the communication obtains a valid authorization from the recipient of the communication (valid under the HIPAA Privacy Rule) with respect to that communication
  - The communication is made by a business associate on behalf of the covered entity
  - The communication is consistent with the written contract (or other written arrangement described in Section 164.502(e)(2) of the Privacy Rule) between the business associate and covered entity

It will be up to the Secretary to define what is "reasonable" in amount, through future regulation.

This section of ARRA also calls on the Secretary to issue regulations noting that any written fundraising communication that is considered a "healthcare operation" shall offer an opportunity for recipients to opt out of receiving future communications. The opt-out option must be "clear and conspicuous." Once a recipient opts out, their decision must be treated as a revocation of authorization for fundraising communications in the future.

The provisions of this marketing and fundraising section of ARRA apply to written communications occurring on or after February 17, 2010.

## Enforcement Provisions

One area in which ARRA has taken HIPAA to an entirely new level is in the area of enforcement and penalties. Although there were some enforcement activities under HIPAA, and authority for enforcement activities has always been present, actual enforcement activities were infrequent. The initial approach to HIPAA enforcement was educational in nature, while the healthcare industry became familiar with HIPAA's privacy and security requirements. Now that several years have passed, one could say that the gloves are off, and ARRA takes a more aggressive stance toward privacy and security enforcement.

One of the popular legal debates pre-ARRA centered on the authority to pursue criminal penalties against individuals, since HIPAA was originally designed to cover only "covered entities." Section 13409 of ARRA amends the part of the Social Security Act dealing with possible criminal penalties for the wrongful disclosure of individually identifiable health information. The amendment states that "a person (including an employee or other individual) shall be considered to have obtained or disclosed individually identifiable health information in violation of this part if the information is maintained by a covered entity and the individual obtained or disclosed such information without authorization" (ARRA Section 13409). This makes it clear that criminal penalties can indeed be pursued against individuals.

ARRA increases civil monetary penalty amounts over previous levels, based on the level (or tier) of intent and neglect, such as whether the violation was made without knowledge, due to reasonable cause, or due to willful neglect (refer to figure 2.6.). The Office for Civil Rights (OCR) is still permitted to use corrective action without penalty, but only in situations where the violation was made without knowledge. In all other cases, penalties are mandatory. The penalties collected will be used to support the enforcement activities of the OCR, and individuals whose PHI was the subject of an enforcement action will receive a percentage of any penalties collected. Regulations on distribution of these penalty percentages to harmed individuals must be issued no later than February 17, 2012, but the new enforcement provision take effect for penalties imposed on or after February 17, 2011. Regulations for other aspects of penalty enforcement are due on or about August 17, 2010.

# Key Provisions Impacting the HIPAA Privacy Rules

The current version of HIPAA does not provide a private right of action for harmed individuals. Individuals whose information was breached cannot use HIPAA regulations as a basis to sue. ARRA also does not grant a private right of action, but it does authorize state attorneys general to file suit on behalf of their residents. The state is required to notify the Secretary prior to any such action, and the suit cannot proceed if the Secretary already has an enforcement action underway.

Section 13411 requires the Secretary to perform periodic audits to ensure that covered entities and business associates are complying with the rules. This is a change, as the prior approach was largely complaint-driven. As a result, covered entities are highly likely to see a greater number of enforcement actions.

## Important Provisions for Noncovered Entities

As noted earlier, there are some obligations under ARRA's HITECH provisions for noncovered entities, for example, entities that do not meet the definition of covered entity or business associate under the rules. These can be found in Section 13407, which includes some temporary breach notification requirements directed at vendors of PHRs and other noncovered entities. These requirements apply not only to vendors of PHRs but also to entities:

- Offering products or services through the Web site of a vendor of PHRs; or
- Other than covered entities, that offer products or services through the Web sites of covered entities that offer individuals PHRs; and
- Other than covered entities, that access information in a PHR or send information to a PHR

As mentioned, following the discovery of a breach of information, the entity must notify each individual who is a citizen or resident of the United States whose unsecured PHR identifiable health information was acquired by an authorized person as a result of breach of security. They must also notify the FTC. This provision of ARRA was followed by a final rule on Health Breach Notification, published by the Federal Trade Commission in the August 25, 2009 *Federal Register*.

Third-party service providers to vendors of PHRs or the entities listed earlier must also report breaches of security to the vendor or applicable entity. That notice must include the identification of each individual whose unsecured PHR identifiable health information has been, or is reasonably believe to have been, accessed, acquired, or disclosed during the breach (ARRA Section 13407(b)). These noncovered entity vendors must follow ARRA's breach notification requirements in a manner to be specified by the FTC, and the FTC will notify the HHS Secretary.

Violations of ARRA by these noncovered entities will be treated as unfair and deceptive acts or practices in violation of regulations promulgated under the Federal Trade Commission Act.

The definition of a *breach of security* for these kinds of noncovered entities has been specifically listed in this section of ARRA (13407(f)). A breach of security means, with respect to unsecured

PHR identifiable health information of an individual in a PHR, "acquisition of such information without the authorization of the individual." This is not the same as the breach definition governing covered entities and business associates; this definition is not qualified with exceptions.

"PHR identifiable health information" has also been defined in Section 13407(f). It means individually identifiable health information as defined by HIPAA that is provided by or on behalf of the individual *and* identifies the individual (or for which there is a reasonable basis to believe that the information can be used to identify the individual).

As noted earlier, this section of ARRA will require privacy compliance by a new class of entities that are not covered entities under HIPAA. With this section, ARRA's HITECH provisions take a large step in expanding the scope of federal privacy and security protections.

## Education on Health Information Privacy

With all of these changes, we're all likely to see and experience a good deal of confusion as the healthcare industry and others become more familiar with the rules. It's also likely there will be some public confusion and concern. Congress anticipated this and has provided for privacy education programs in Section 13403 of ARRA. Within six months of ARRA enactment, the HHS Secretary must designate an individual—a privacy advisor—in each regional office of HHS. This person is to offer guidance and education to covered entities, business associates, and individuals on their rights and responsibilities related to federal privacy and security requirements for protected health information. Privacy officers were designated for each regional office in August 2009.

By February 17, 2010, the Office for Civil Rights must develop a multifaceted national education initiative to enhance public transparency regarding uses of PHI. This education will include programs on potential uses of PHI, effects of such uses, and individual rights. Congress has directed OCR to offer this education in a variety of languages and to present the information in a clear and understandable manner. Some of these materials and information may be useful to covered entities in working directly with their patients and clients, as well, so this initiative bears watching as it develops.

## References

American Health Information Management Association. March 2009. *Analysis of Health Care Confidentiality, Privacy, and Security Provisions of the American Recovery and Reinvestment Act of 2009, Public Law 111-5.* www.ahima.org/dc/documents/AnalysisofARRAPrivacy-fin-3-2009a.pdf.

American Recovery and Reinvestment Act of 2009. Public Law 111-5.

Department of Health and Human Services. 2009a. Health Information Technology. Health IT Home. http://healthit.hhs.gov.

Department of Health and Human Services. 2009b (August 24). Interim final rule: Breach notification for unsecured protected health information. *Federal Register.*

Federal Trade Commission. 2009 (August 25). Final rule: Health breach notification rule. *Federal Register.*

Gellman, R. 2009. Notes and Observations on Selected Parts of Title XIII, Subtitle D, Privacy. http://www.bobgellman.com/rg-docs/Stimulus-Privacy-HIPAA-Analysis.pdf.

45 CFR Subpart E: Privacy of individually identifiable health information. 2000, 2002.

45 CFR 160, 162, and 164: Health insurance reform: Security standards. 2003.

# Chapter 3

# Operational Challenges

What are going to be the challenges associated with implementing ARRA's HITECH changes to the HIPAA privacy and security regulations? If you are involved in compliance preparations and planning, what do you need to keep in mind as you begin your work? What areas of the new rules have hidden, or not-so-hidden, landmines from an operational point of view? That is the focus of this chapter. Chapter 4, Implementation Strategies, begins to address the challenges and questions introduced here.

## Who Needs to Know What

One of the first operational challenges in dealing with any regulatory change is embedding knowledge of the new rules within one's organization, as needed. The entire workforce does not need to be privacy or security experts, but everyone needs to know certain basics. This was true during HIPAA implementation, and it is true of ARRA as well. Sorting out who needs to know what is going to make that job easier and will avoid overdosing staff with levels of detail that may not be necessary. Many organizations approach this issue by literally defining the changes that must be taught and overlaying that information onto a list of workforce and provider staff categories based on how they typically interact with health information.

This approach results in a simple grid that can be used to plan and customize education, where possible, for those groups. Even within a single role or staff category, there are some real differences in the amount of information different subgroups may need. For example, to tackle the issue of breaches—what they are? what happens when one occurs? what are the penalties? how is the patient informed? who is responsible for breach notification? and what should one do if a breach is suspected?—it is useful to consider how the needs might differ for a typical hospital, based on categories of staff such as these listed here. Some of the categories are expanded to illustrate how different subgroups may have different needs.

- Medical staff
    - Hospitalists (with daily, heavy contact with patient information)
    - General active staff
    - Consulting staff/remote/telehealth (special security issues associated with off-site access to information)
- Employed nursing staff
    - Floor staff
    - Emergency Department (heavy phone contact with the public)
    - Surgery staff and special procedures areas
- Temporary care provider staff such as locum tenens, travelers, PRN nurses, consultants, and such (what are they key things they need to know for their brief time on site?)
- Other care provider/therapist employees; including contract staff
- Non-care employees with access to patient information
    - Housekeeping/environmental services
    - Maintenance
    - Other
- Health information management staff
    - Release of information coordinators
    - Remote coders, transcriptionists
    - General
- Patient accounting/billing/finance
- Patient access/registration/preregistration staff
- Information technology staff
    - Information security staff
    - Help desk
    - Other
- Marketing staff
- Fundraising/foundation staff
- Executive/public relations staff

Operational Challanges 37

The challenge of embedding necessary knowledge of the new rules in one's organization is not as simple as producing generic ARRA/HITECH education for all. A more effective process will seek to target the education to various groups' needs. This is particularly important in light of our staff members' growing awareness of their potential personal criminal liability under ARRA's HITECH provisions.

## The Rules Are a Moving Target

Unlike many regulatory changes, where there is a single effective date for all changes, ARRA's provisions have differing effective dates for many provisions. There are also varying dates set for the issuance of regulations, not to mention the likelihood of annual updates to various regulations and guidance. This has implications for the organization's training efforts and will force certain priorities to be set during planning. Matching an organization's policy and procedure development to the applicable effective dates can help spread out the workload as well. Table 3.1 lists effective dates for various sections of ARRA's privacy and security provisions.

Table 3.1. Important effective dates and expected regulations for ARRA/HITECH*

| Provision or Expected Regulation | Due | Effective Date |
|---|---|---|
| All provisions without a separately designated effective date | | February 17, 2010 |
| Request for additional funding, authority, legislation, and such, including privacy and security (Section 3001) | February 17, 2010 | |
| Appointment of Chief Privacy Officer for ONC | February 17, 2010 | |
| Appointment of HIT Policy Committee | Completed | |
| Schedule for assessment of policy recommendations by HIT Standards Committee | Completed | |
| Guidance on most effective and appropriate technologies for security (to be issued by Secretary) (Section 13401) | February 17, 2010 | |
| Guidance specifying the technologies and methodologies to render PHI unusable (Section 13402) | Completed | |

Table 3.1. Important effective dates and expected regulations for ARRA/HITECH* *(continued)*

| Provision or Expected Regulation | Due | Effective Date |
|---|---|---|
| Breach report to Congress from Secretary (Section 13402) | February 17, 2010 | |
| Interim final rules on breach requirements for HIPAA entities (Section 13402) | Completed August 24, 2009 | September 23, 2009 (with six-month delay in sanction application) |
| HHS regional offices to designate privacy officers to provide guidance and education on privacy and security (Section 13403) | Done | |
| HHS develops education initiative to enhance public transparency regarding uses of PHI, rights, and the like (Section 13403) | February 17, 2010 | |
| Limited data set to be considered for use until guidance on minimum necessary is issued (Section 13405) | | February 17, 2010, sunsets with effective date of guidance on minimum necessary |
| Guidance on "minimum necessary" | August 17, 2010 | To be set by HHS |
| Regulation on data to be provided for accounting of disclosures, related to EHRs (Section 13405) | Six months after Secretary adopts standards on accounting | Varies with when EHR is acquired, see 13405(c)(4) |
| Regulation related to prohibition on sale of PHI/EHRs (Section 13405) | August 17, 2010 | February 17, 2011 |
| Marketing: Definition of "reasonable in amount" (Section 13406) | | February 17, 2010 or after |
| "Opt Out" of fundraising clarification (Section 13406) | | February 17, 2010 or after |
| Interim final rule: breaches by vendors of PHRs and other noncovered entities (Section 13407) | Completed; published as Final rule on August 25, 2009 | Applies to breaches on or after September 24, 2009 |

| | | |
|---|---|---|
| "Willful neglect" regulations (Section 13410) | August 17, 2010 | Will apply to penalties imposed on or after February 17, 2011 |
| Report on distribution of penalties collected (Section 13410) | August 17, 2010 | |
| Regulation on revised distribution of penalties (Section 13410) | Between August 17, 2010 and February 17, 2012 | Will take effect for penalties imposed on/after February 17, 2011 |
| Tiered increase in amounts of civil monetary penalties (Section 13410) | | February 17, 2009 |
| Enforcement by State Attorneys General (Section 13410) | | February 17, 2009 |
| Report on Compliance with ARRA and HIPAA to Congress | By February 17, 2010, then annually | |
| Study, report on application of privacy/security requirements to noncovered entities to Congress | By February 17, 2010 | |
| Guidance on implementation specification to deidentify PHI (Section 13424) | By February 17, 2010 | |
| GAO report on best practices for treatment disclosures | By February 17, 2010 | |
| Study: definition of psychotherapy notes | Unspecified | |

Source: AHIMA 2009.

*ARRA was enacted on February 17, 2009. Effective dates in the various provisions are linked to the overall effective dates. This table also lists the dates Congress set for the issuance of clarifying regulations by the Secretary of HHS. These timetables are subject to change.*

## Breaches Will Be Numerous

ARRA's provisions on breaches will cast a very wide net and require a good deal of notification. Notifications will be costly both in terms of labor and good will. Despite years of familiarity with HIPAA, there are frequent reports of "snooping" behavior, where covered entity staff look up data on celebrities, friends, and family members. This has always been wrong, but now the consequences are potentially even more serious. It will be difficult to focus on privacy and security improvements if an organization has not yet addressed these typical kinds of breaches.

This subject must be addressed now through staff education, policy tightening, and consistent enforcement of the rules across the organization. Those privacy and security officers who set this problem aside will be hard-pressed to find sufficient time later to address other aspects of the changed provisions.

## The Need for New or Revised Policies and Procedures

Even when a business process already exists for a provision covered by ARRA, substantial changes may be needed. The accounting of disclosures process is an excellent example. All covered entities already have a process developed. However, if they have an electronic health record (EHR), and if they make certain disclosures through the electronic record (specifically, treatment, payment, and healthcare operations-related disclosures), those disclosures will have to appear on the accounting. This will require a good deal of staff education, as well as a mechanism to log (or communicate to a central party who then logs the disclosure) as those kinds of disclosures are made. Will the electronic record have a way of automatically documenting or logging those disclosures? If not, some sort of manual process for logging these disclosures will be needed. How long will that information be retained? Will it be available to the privacy officer if and when an individual requests an accounting? How will that information be blended with previously trackable disclosures (under the HIPAA Privacy Rule) that do not occur through an electronic record? The questions are easy; the solutions will require some work.

Many business associates will likely be taking on the responsibility for providing an accounting directly to the patient (for their disclosures). It is likely that some covered entities will elect to take advantage of the option, under Section 13405 of ARRA, to require their business associate to account directly to the patient for applicable disclosures by the business associate, and if so, it will be important to specify that arrangement in the business associate agreement. If this option is exercised, it will require a new business process. And it is very likely that business associates who deal with multiple covered entities will need to have multiple approaches based on the preferences of their clients: some covered entities may want to continue handling the accounting in a centralized way; others may be more than happy to refer individuals directly to the business associate.

Another new process for many business associates will be necessary to comply with ARRA Section 13404(b). Under the HIPAA Privacy Rule (45 CFR Subpart E Section 164.504(e)(1)(ii)) covered entities are required to take action if they are aware of a business associate's noncompliance with the business associate agreement. Under this provision of ARRA, business associates who become aware of a pattern of activity, or practice, of the covered entity that constitutes a material breach or violation must take action. Unless reasonable and successful steps are taken to cure the breach or end the violation, the business associate must terminate their agreement with the covered entity, or if that is not feasible, they must report the problem to the Secretary.

Vendors of personal health records (PHRs) and other noncovered entities will also be writing new policies and procedures. Section 13407 and FTC regulations issued in August 2009 require breach notification when a breach of security occurs, and this section of the rule has specific requirements for how and to whom that notification takes place. This is a new business process for most of the organizations covered by this section. Complicating compliance preparation will be the fact that these organizations may have been relatively unfamiliar with federal privacy and security requirements before ARRA. In addition, there is active debate surrounding whether the FTC's definition of "third-party service providers" in the Health Breach Notification Regulations applies to "host sites" that rent server space to PHR vendors and therefore have access to PHR-identifiable health information.

The ARRA provision on requests to restrict certain disclosures will require some revised business processes for covered entities. Section 13405(a)(1) and (2) will require covered entities to have special procedures for disclosing information when an individual has fully paid for care or service out of pocket, rather than through health insurance. There will need to be ways to specially "flag" or call attention to the information that was paid for, so this information will not be disclosed to the individual's health plan. Given that this could apply to only one test or encounter in a much larger record, or to an entire record, this process will have to be thought through carefully and will have to incorporate the nuances of the exception in this section for treatment-related disclosures.

Covered entities with electronic records will need to investigate methods of providing individuals with electronic copies of that information. What are the options for copying and conveying that information: secure e-mail? by handing the patient a CD or DVD? What is possible? Some patients may want to bring in their own USB drives and have you copy information directly onto it—will this be acceptable from a security point of view? Will you use encryption when sharing electronic copies and give the patient a password? Once these questions are answered, covered entities will need to fully understand the labor costs involved with each option, since that will determine what can be charged to the requesting individual (in concert with any other laws that may apply, such as state laws defining copy costs).

ARRA's limited data set provisions will also require revised business processes. Persons disclosing protected health information (PHI) will have to routinely consider whether restricting the information disclosed to meet the standards of a limited data set would accomplish the purpose of that disclosure. If so, the data contained in the disclosure must be stripped of the elements not permitted in a limited data set. This will essentially be a new first step in making disclosures. Given that a wide range of persons make disclosures of PHI in any covered entity, this step will affect numerous departments and will require a good deal of staff education.

Many covered entities experienced difficulties in understanding the HIPAA Privacy Rules governing marketing and fundraising when those rules were first issued. With the revisions in ARRA, policies and procedures in those business areas will need to be reviewed for needed revisions, and those staff will need to be updated on the changes.

## Business Associate Agreement Revisions

There are at least two schools of thought on whether all business associate agreements will need to be revised by the compliance date. Some lawyers advise specifically incorporating all the new business associate obligations under ARRA's HITECH provisions into the business associate agreement, which would require amending current agreements. Others advise looking at the current language in the business associate agreement, and if it already requires the business associate to comply with all applicable current and future laws and regulations, there may be no need for change. However, given the expanded responsibilities of business associates under ARRA, relying on generic clauses requiring compliance with all current and future laws and regulations could pose a greater risk of confusion and misunderstanding between covered entities and their business associates.

Section 13401 is not entirely clear on the point. It states that the requirements "shall be incorporated into the business associate agreement between the business associate and the covered entity" (ARRA Section 13401(a)). Does this require specific, point-by-point incorporation of the business associate's new obligations or a more generic obligation to comply with existing and future laws suffice? This is a question covered entities and business associates will have to decide with legal counsel, and it is a question that must be answered soon, given the amount of work involved in redrafting and amending the agreements. It is not at all unusual for even small covered entities to have hundreds of business associates. They may range from large national companies with their own legal and compliance staffs, to small sole proprietorships with relatively few resources to monitor, understand, and incorporate these new obligations into their own operations. Given the scope of changes that ARRA brings to business associates, this may be a time in which covered entities should be evaluating their business associate's ability to adequately safeguard PHI.

## Ongoing Challenges with Preemption Analysis

ARRA's privacy provisions use a similar approach to preemption as found in HIPAA. ARRA will only preempt "contrary" state laws. If one can comply with both ARRA's provisions *and* the state law, one must. As a result, for those in states with extensive privacy legislation or regulation, such as breach reporting requirements, covered entities will once again be engaged in preemption analyses to determine what provisions they must follow. As was true under HIPAA, these efforts can best be accomplished through cooperative work with others in the same state. It would be wise to identify any plans for such an analysis and take advantage of any such efforts.

## References

American Health Information Management Association (AHIMA) 2009. Analysis of ARRA Privacy. http://www.ahima.org/arra.

American Recovery and Reinvestment Act of 2009. Public Law 111-5.

Federal Trade Commission. 2009 (August 25). Final rule: Health breach notification rule. *Federal Register.*

45 CFR Subpart E: Privacy of individually identifiable health information. 2000, 2002.

# Chapter 4

# Implementation Strategies

If you've already familiarized yourself with how ARRA's HITECH Act impacts HIPAA's Privacy and Security Rules, you're probably already considering how to tackle this considerable challenge. The healthcare industry has gone through these types of challenges many times before, and past implementation experiences with HIPAA should serve healthcare entities well as they gear up for these changes. This chapter explores some practical strategies for breaking that challenge down into more manageable pieces. It's true that not all of the provisions are immediately effective. And most covered entities (and even business associates) are not starting from scratch. However, for these same reasons, organizations must guard against complacency. There is plenty to do, and it's time to get started.

Perhaps the best way to implement the various changes brought on by ARRA is to take the change management advice of well-known business author John Kotter who describes an eight-stage change process in his book *Leading Change* (Kotter 1996, 21):

1. Establish a sense of urgency
2. Create the guiding coalition
3. Develop a vision and strategy
4. Communicate the change vision
5. Empower broad-based action
6. Generate short-term wins
7. Consolidate gains and produce more change
8. Anchor new approaches in the culture

This chapter doesn't discuss these steps in detail, but it is easy to see how they relate to the change management process.

## Implementing Change

In some ways, a sense of urgency is supported by the amount of attention devoted to these changes in the healthcare industry press. By the same token, staff tend to grow weary of the "next big thing" and may rebel against the seemingly constant barrage of new mandates. The goal isn't to create staff panic, but covered entities need to get and keep staff attention on the issue of privacy and security compliance. So, consider how to help build that sense of urgency in your organization. Kotter tells us that "creating a strong sense of urgency usually demands bold or even risky actions that we normally associate with good leadership" (Kotter 1996, 42–43). If an organization has experienced a privacy or security breach, they might consider inviting that patient or client to talk at a staff education program about how they were affected by that breach. Getting and keeping the staff's attention might require some creativity.

## Guide the Change Process

Organization-wide change isn't easy to achieve or sustain. Don't jeopardize the odds for successful ARRA/HITECH implementation by turning over responsibility for implementation to a committee without sufficient power and influence to make things happen. Kotter urges consideration of four key characteristics when building an effective coalition to guide change (Kotter 1996, 57):

- **Position power:** Are enough key players on board, especially the main line managers, so that those left out cannot easily block progress?

- **Expertise:** Are the various points of view (in terms of discipline, work experience, and such) relevant to the task at hand adequately represented?

- **Credibility:** Does the group have enough people with good reputations, so that its pronouncements will be taken seriously?

- **Leadership:** Does the group include enough proven leaders to be able to drive the change?

If these characteristics match up well with the HIPAA team from years ago that worked to implement HIPAA's changes, the organization may have a head start. Of all staff members, these individuals are probably most conversant with fundamental privacy and security principles. However, take into account whether that team needs to be supplemented to meet the criteria listed earlier. Are new parties needed? Are current parties no longer needed?

Consider, as well, whether this team has the project management skills and tools that will facilitate bringing the necessary changes in on time. The law has varying and staggered effective dates, and different departments and subsets of the organization will be involved in various aspects of compliance. Implementing these changes will be somewhat complex and will require good documentation of the decision-making process. In fact, that documentation will be especially important for business associates who will be complying with HIPAA's security regulations for the first time and will therefore engage in decisions about the "addressable" security implementation specifications. Those decisions' rationales will need to be maintained in the event those decisions are challenged.

## Divide Up the Work

Implementation of the new provisions will require a number of changes to business policies and practices. If all policies and procedures are being rewritten by a single individual (or the same handful of individuals), that's probably a good sign of an implementation destined for failure. After the HIPAA Privacy Rule was announced, publishers came out of the woodwork to offer boilerplate policy and procedure manuals to "ensure" compliance with the rules. Other covered entities tended to borrow the policies and procedures of other covered entities and simply change the logos and titles to make it appear that this was their own. The problems with these boilerplates and borrowed materials are:

- They probably don't reflect each organization's reality, which limits their value as guidance to staff.

- Because they don't reflect reality, they're not useful in supporting disciplinary actions or sanctions taken against those who violate the standards they contain.

- When the discrepancies between these documents and actual practice are discovered as part of litigation or enforcement actions, it reflects poorly on the organization and makes staff actions more difficult to defend or justify.

- An organization is trusting that the author really understands the underlying laws and regulations. That trust may or may not be justified.

Although it can be instructive to have a starting point when writing policies and procedures, it's vital that these reflect actual and expected practices of each organization. Use them with caution and only after they have been reality-tested with affected staff. An organization's workflow, culture, and staff characteristics should drive these documents, along with the requirements of the law. That probably means involving a variety of managers and staff in actually drafting procedures and then having a more centralized process for checking for compliance with all applicable laws and regulations.

## Set Priorities

This implementation process is multifaceted, and change doesn't happen overnight. And, of course, these changes must be implemented while still taking care of normal day-to-day responsibilities. Some of the changes may be relatively quick and simple; others will take a longer period of time. Decide what to do first, second, and third. Create a logical sequence of tasks, as some tasks have dependencies that will require other tasks to already be complete.

As mentioned, a team member with solid project management skills will be important in helping to prioritize the tasks. And the law itself may offer some useful clues about what must begin now versus what can wait.

### Check the Effective Dates

Although many provisions take effect on February 17, 2010, not all of them do. Refer to table 3.1 for specific deadlines. Know what will be required to implement the necessary changes, and work backward from the effective dates to determine when key tasks must be started and when certain milestones must be met.

### Consider the Risks

Of course, all aspects of privacy and security compliance are important, but some areas are likely to pose greater risks. The list may vary from organization to organization based on past practices, resources, and culture, but educating staff about what qualifies as a "breach" should be high on the list. The sheer volume of people with access to health information probably makes this an important priority in most organizations handling health information.

### Consider the Unknown

For those aspects of the law where there is no official guidance, it probably makes good sense to postpone finalizing the business process changes, policies, staff education, and any other associated preparations, if the effective dates of those provisions permit delay. Keep in mind, however, that all parties subject to the law and regulations are still responsible for meeting any applicable effective dates, even if important compliance guidance (or even clarifying regulations) are delayed.

### Decide On a Business Associate Contracting Strategy

Someone needs to make some decisions fairly quickly, because there are probably a large number of these agreements, and they will take time to review and renegotiate (if needed). Here are some of the questions to consider:

- Is it necessary to amend all existing business associate agreements, or does legal counsel believe the existing language covers the organization on the new requirements?

- Is there a need to continue accounting for the disclosures made by business associates (as applicable), or will persons requesting an accounting of those disclosures be referred directly to the business associates via a list?

- Are the business associates aware of and able to follow the provisions applicable to them?

- If business associates struggle to comply, will there be a need to begin looking at alternative vendors?

- Will the organization insist on using our preferred language for new or revised business associate agreements, or will the business associates be allowed to write these agreements?

- If the organization accepts the business associates' written agreements, is there an effective process for reviewing and approving those agreements?

## Consider Electronic Record Capabilities

Some of the provisions of ARRA are less burdensome if an organization's electronic records have certain capabilities. For example, keeping an accounting log or record of treatment, payment, and healthcare operations-related disclosures through an EHR becomes a fairly simple process if the EHR is designed to easily track these disclosures. That information can be blended with the accounting of other types of disclosures and provided to the individual upon request. Covered entities need to explore this issue with their vendor to see how the software can assist in implementation and compliance efforts.

## Review Privacy and Security Compliance

Covered entities have had to comply with HIPAA's privacy and security regulations for some time now. Some organizations do an excellent job of self-auditing and periodically examining their own internal compliance with those roles. Others have probably drifted somewhat from the practices mandated by the regulations and their own internal policies. Given that enforcement activities are ratcheting up to include periodic audits, this is a good time to take a look at the current status of privacy- and security-related practices. Don't assume that what's written in the policies and procedures is actually what's happening. There are a number of good resources available on auditing compliance. Some Web-based resources can be found in appendix B on the CD-ROM that accompanies this book.

## Field-Test Draft Policies and Procedures

Before finalizing any new or revised policies and procedures, be sure to invite affected staff to do a quick reality check. Here are some questions to use as part of this process:

- Is this what the organization really wants staff to do?

- Can the staff do it? Will they?

- Does this policy or procedure meet all applicable requirements, for example, ARRA, state privacy laws, and the like?

- Is there a better way to accomplish the objective?

- For procedures, have the steps been clearly defined?

- Are all the steps necessary, or are they simply "the way it has always been done"?

- Would a process flowchart or diagram be simpler for staff to follow than words on a page?

- What should a staff member do if he or she has a better idea?

- What should a staff member do if he or she discovers obstacles to following a policy or procedure?

## Avoid Canned Policies and Procedures

As mentioned in chapter 3, watching out for canned policies and procedures is important, especially if you have a large number of people involved in writing them. As it was during the HIPAA implementation period, there is likely to be an influx of ARRA boilerplate policy and procedures manuals available for purchase. It's best to avoid the "one-size-fits-all" policies and procedures.

## Know the Retention Requirements

As the organization revises existing practices and develops new ones, don't forget there are retention requirements for documents that pertain to privacy and security compliance (generally, but not universally, six years). As policies and procedures change, how will an organization know what policy or procedure is effective at any given point in time? Someone in the organization must be prepared to retain prior versions of policies and procedures for at least the minimum required retention period. A good practice is to file copies of each version with an annotation that reflects both the effective (starting) date and the expiration date. Centralizing these is not required, but can make retrieval much simpler if these documents become relevant in audits, investigations, discovery, or litigation.

## Make Policies and Procedures Readily Available

Before computers, it was common to find voluminous three-ring binders in various departments and on patient-care units. They were cumbersome, and it's not surprising that they weren't always used or kept current. An organization still using paper binders should test that theory by sampling the contents from one of the organization's departments: How many expired items are still in there? Have any been informally (and unofficially) revised through the handwritten addition of steps, sticky notes, and the like? How dusty are the pages? Is anything missing? Today's increasingly common practice of putting those documents on the intranet for easy (and read-only) access by staff (and with the added benefit of search capabilities) is a better solution. Whatever the choice, be sure that the finalized policies and procedures are readily available to all the staff that need them. This is important at any time, but particularly when a policy or procedure is new or changed, since staff will need to access those documents more frequently.

## Start Thinking about Workforce Training

Chapter 3 discusses one approach to deciding who needs to know what. Organizations are free to use any approach that works well, but that's the key—what is going to work *well*? Neither ARRA nor HIPAA dictate how to approach workforce training. Consider the options for delivering this content—not everything has to be accompanied by a PowerPoint slide show and the inevitable handout. If these work well for staff, by all means use them. But keep your goal in mind: comprehension, understanding, and adoption of any needed changes in behavior.

Also consider options for timing this training. How useful will this information be if it is delivered months in advance of actually using that information? How useful will it be if it is delivered after the effective date in the regulations for that particular issue? What information needs to be kept fresh in the minds of your staff—and so should be repeated or refreshed at intervals? Remember, too, that new guidances and regulations will be issued well into the future, and those items may have training implications as well. Ongoing staff education will be an important ingredient in the successful implementation of these changes.

## Don't Forget the Public Dimension of Privacy and Security

For the near-term future, covered entities, business associates, personal health record (PHR) vendors, and other types of organizations mentioned in ARRA will be coming to terms with the changes associated with this law and its regulations—and so will the public. Therefore, this presents an opportunity to provide a valuable public service to those individuals whose health information you manage. ARRA gives individuals some new rights. Can your organization help them understand their new options? What should the public know about requesting restrictions or requesting information in electronic formats? Are there things individuals can do to better protect their own health information once they receive a copy? What should they expect when they request an accounting of disclosures? What should they do if they suspect a breach? And what can they expect from your organization if a breach occurs? These questions would all be good topics for public education about health information, privacy and security, and individual rights.

When the worst happens, and a breach occurs, ARRA requires notification of the individual(s) whose information has been breached. The minimum elements of a breach notification letter are specified in the law, as discussed in chapter 2, but it's also important to consider the tone of that letter. The covered entity's goal should be not only to meet the requirement of law but to assist the individual and begin to repair the breach of trust that can accompany this event. Medical and risk management literature documents growth in the use of apologies (as well as in state apology laws) in acknowledging untoward patient care events and errors (Dresser 2008, 6). Consider the tone as breach notification letters are drafted.

It has been common for covered entities to routinely refuse all patient requests for restrictions, due to often legitimate concerns about whether that request could be consistently honored. Under ARRA's provision requiring the covered entity to honor requested restrictions on disclosures to health plans of information that have already been paid for in full by the patient (except treatment disclosures), the policy of blanket denials must be revised, whether it was a written or unwritten rule. And as EHR systems become more sophisticated and capable of sorting data using various filters, covered entities' ability to reliably and consistently handle restrictions should improve. More patient-friendly restriction capabilities should build individuals' confidence in the privacy of health information and in the covered entities that are handling patient information.

Similarly, with the new right of individuals to request copies of their health information in electronic format (if the covered entity maintains an electronic record), there is an opportunity to educate the public about the need for safe practices in maintaining their own health information. For example, the requesting individual could be told about the advantages and disadvantages of various available formats from a security point of view.

The implementation team should also consider whether any of these changes warrant revisions to the organization's notice of privacy practices. Although ARRA is silent as to changes in the notice, covered entities have an ongoing responsibility under the HIPAA Privacy Rule to keep that notice current (see HIPAA Privacy Rule, Section 164.530(i)(2)(ii)). For example, language about the individual's right to request restrictions, and that the covered entity is not required to agree, would be an example of common privacy notice elements that would need updating.

Implementation of the ARRA changes will require considerable time and effort, but they also offer an opportunity to improve an organization's ability to serve as trusted stewards of protected health information and further the public's acceptance of EHRs.

## References

Dresser, R. 2008. The limits of apology laws. *Hastings Center Report* 38(3):6.

Kotter, J. P. 1996. *Leading Change.* Boston, MA: Harvard Business School Press.

45 CFR Subpart E. Privacy of Individually Identifiable Health Information. 2000, 2002.

# Chapter 5

# Impact beyond the HIPAA Privacy and Security Rules

The main thrust of the privacy and security provisions of ARRA's HITECH Act is to strengthen the protections for health information, primarily (although not solely) through amendments to HIPAA's Privacy and Security Rules. As noted, the scope of ARRA/HITECH goes beyond what already existed in HIPAA to extend privacy and security obligations to certain noncovered entities. For example, there are breach of security notification provisions applicable to vendors of personal health records (PHRs) and certain third-party service providers (discussed in chapter 2).

## State Laws

Another aspect of ARRA's impact beyond the existing HIPAA rules can be found in state privacy and security laws. Post-HIPAA, a number of states passed privacy legislation that is more stringent (or privacy-protective) than HIPAA. Many states are now wondering how the privacy- and security-related provisions of ARRA will interact with these laws. Unfortunately, the answer is not yet completely clear, but most observers believe that the preemption analysis approach taken under HIPAA will still, be useful under ARRA. It is one of the unresolved questions covered in chapter 6. Suffice it to say here that compliance and implementation plans should be examining not only ARRA's impact on HIPAA, but also how ARRA compares to applicable state laws and regulations. Until the dust has settled on the preemption debate, the wise strategy is to design affected programs, such as breach notification, to meet both standards by meeting the highest (most stringent) requirement.

## The Role of the Federal Trade Commission

ARRA also strengthens the visibility of the role of the Federal Trade Commission (FTC) on matters related to privacy of health information. It obliges the FTC to notify the HHS Secretary of breaches of security reported by PHR vendors and the third-party service providers covered by

Section 13407 (ARRA Section 13407(d)). To ensure this section is carried out, ARRA directed the FTC to issue regulations on this topic, and they were published in the August 25, 2009 *Federal Register*. ARRA also defines violations of Section 13407(a) and (b) as an "unfair and deceptive act or practice in violation of" regulations under the Federal Trade Commission Act. The August 25th regulations also consider violations to be unfair and deceptive acts or practices. The role of the FTC with respect to the privacy and security of health information is not new with this provision—consumer protection is part of their mission, but that role appears to be growing more active and visible. The FTC's case against CVS Caremark is a good example of this, and the press release FTC issued describing the case's resolution can be found in figure 5.1. This was the first healthcare case brought by the FTC.

**Figure 5.1.** FTC press release February 18, 2009

### CVS CAREMARK SETTLES FTC CHARGES:
Failed to Protect Medical and Financial Privacy of Customers and Employees; CVS Pharmacy Also Pays $2.25 Million to Settle Allegations of HIPAA Violations

CVS Caremark has agreed to settle Federal Trade Commission charges that it failed to take reasonable and appropriate security measures to protect the sensitive financial and medical information of its customers and employees, in violation of federal law. In a separate but related agreement, the company's pharmacy chain also has agreed to pay $2.25 million to resolve Department of Health and Human Services allegations that it violated the Health Insurance Portability and Accountability Act (HIPAA).

"This is a case that will restore appropriate privacy protections to tens of millions of people across the country," said William E. Kovacic, Chairman of the Federal Trade Commission. "It also sends a strong message to other organizations that possess consumers' protected personal information. They are required to secure consumers' private information."

CVS Caremark operates the largest pharmacy chain in the United States, with more than 6,300 retail outlets and online and mail-order pharmacy businesses.

The FTC opened its investigation into CVS Caremark following media reports from around the country that its pharmacies were throwing trash into open dumpsters that contained pill bottles with patient names, addresses, prescribing physicians' names, medication and dosages; medication instruction sheets with personal information; computer order information from the pharmacies, including consumers' personal information; employment applications, including social security numbers; payroll information; and credit card and insurance card information, including, in some cases, account numbers and driver's license numbers. At the same time,

HHS opened its investigation into the pharmacies' disposal of health information protected by HIPAA. The FTC and HHS coordinated their investigations and settlements.

The FTC's complaint charges that CVS Caremark failed to implement reasonable and appropriate procedures for handling personal information about customers and employees, in violation of federal laws. In particular, according to the complaint, CVS Caremark did not implement reasonable policies and procedures to dispose securely of personal information, did not adequately train employees, did not use reasonable measures to assess compliance with its policies and procedures for disposing of personal information, and did not employ a reasonable process for discovering and remedying risks to personal information.

CVS Caremark made claims such as "CVS/pharmacy wants you to know that nothing is more central to our operations than maintaining the privacy of your health information." The FTC alleged that the claim was deceptive and that CVS Caremark's security practices also were unfair. Unfair and deceptive practices violate the FTC Act.

The FTC order requires CVS Caremark to establish, implement, and maintain a comprehensive information security program designed to protect the security, confidentiality, and integrity of the personal information it collects from consumers and employees. It also requires the company to obtain, every two years for the next 20 years, an audit from a qualified, independent, third-party professional to ensure that its security program meets the standards of the order. CVS Caremark will be subject to standard record-keeping and reporting provisions to allow the FTC to monitor compliance. Finally, the settlement bars future misrepresentations of the company's security practices.

The HHS settlement requires CVS pharmacies to establish and implement policies and procedures for disposing of protected health information, implement a training program for handling and disposing of such patient information, conduct internal monitoring, and engage an outside independent assessor to evaluate compliance for three years. CVS also will pay HHS $2.25 million to settle the matter.

The Commission vote to accept the proposed consent agreement was 4-0. The FTC will publish an announcement regarding the agreement in the Federal Register shortly. The agreement will be subject to public comment for 30 days, beginning today and continuing through March 20, 2009, after which the Commission will decide whether to make it final. Comments should be addressed to the FTC, Office of the Secretary, Room H-135, 600 Pennsylvania Avenue, N.W., Washington, DC 20580. The FTC is requesting that any comment filed in paper form near the end of the public comment period be sent by courier or overnight service, if possible, because U.S. postal mail in the Washington area and at the Commission is subject to delay due to heightened security precautions.

Source: FTC 2009.

## State Attorneys General and Civil Actions

Section 13410's grant of authority to state attorneys general to bring civil actions if a resident of that state has been or is threatened or adversely affected by violations of ARRA's HITECH provisions is also a step beyond HIPAA. It opens up a new source of potential liability for covered entities and business associates, and provides added pressure and incentive to comply with the rules.

## Impact on EHR Availability

Finally, privacy and security provisions aside, remember that one of the main purposes of ARRA's provisions related to the healthcare industry is to improve care and reduce costs through further adoption of health information technology. This should spur growth in the availability—and capability—of electronic health records and related health IT applications. As the percentage of U.S. health information that is stored electronically grows, this will raise the need and demand for more secure systems.

## References

American Recovery and Reinvestment Act of 2009. Public Law 111-5.

Federal Trade Commission. 2009. Press release: CVS Caremark Settles FTC Charges. February 2009. http://www.hhs.gov/news/press/2009pres/02/20090218a.html.

Federal Trade Commission. 2009 (August 25). Final rule: Health breach notification rule. *Federal Register*.

15 USC Sections 41–58, as amended. Federal Trade Commission Act of 1914.

# Chapter 6

# Unresolved Questions and Conflicts

Those working in the privacy or security arena during the time in which HIPAA's Privacy and Security Rules were being drafted, debated, and implemented recall the struggles associated with interpreting sections of the rules. Many hours were spent trying to understand the preemption provisions of the rule alone: perhaps not so much the language of the rule itself, but certainly in how that language was applied to various state laws and regulations—and even other federal laws and regulations, such as the Family Educational Rights and Privacy Act (FERPA) and 42 CFR Part 2 (regulations on Confidentiality of Alcohol and Drug Abuse Patient Records).

## State Breach Notification Laws

It appears there will be similar debates with respect to ARRA's impact on state breach notification laws. If one examines ARRA Section 13421, it appears to say that ARRA's approach to preemption will apply in the same manner as HIPAA did. Under HIPAA's provisions, more stringent state privacy laws were not preempted, and Section 13421(a) of ARRA appears to keep this principle. But the American Health Lawyers Association's HIT-listserv has hosted a number of informal electronic debates and posts on this subject. And just as was true during HIPAA implementation, the ultimate answer will depend in part on the specific language within the state's law (for example, is it "contrary" to ARRA resulting, in preemption by ARRA, or is it "more stringent" than ARRA's provisions and therefore prevails?).

Drafting organizational policy while these debates are still underway is a frustrating exercise for those covered by ARRA and these various state laws and rules. In the meantime, perhaps the best strategy is to ensure organizational practices meet the highest applicable standard. This will require the implementation team to be aware of state laws and regulations that touch on privacy and security matters and to consider those as part of the analysis and preparation. Legal counsel should be involved in these preemption discussions.

## Defining Breach

Another area that may require further clarification is the definition of *breach* in Section 13400, which is shown in figure 6.1, and subsequently modified by the August 25th HHS regulations on breach notification.

**Figure 6.1.   ARRA's definition of breach**

The term *breach* means the unauthorized acquisition, access, use, or disclosure of protected health information which compromises the security or privacy of such information, except where an unauthorized person to whom such information is disclosed would not reasonably have been able to retain such information.

*Exceptions*: The term *breach* does not include

- Any unintentional acquisition, access, or use of protected health information by an employee or individual acting under the authority of a covered entity or business associate if
  - Such acquisition, access, or use was made in good faith and within the course and scope of the employment or other professional relationship of such employee or individual, respectively, with the covered entity or business associate; and
  - Such information is not further acquired, accessed, used, or disclosed by any person; or
- Any inadvertent disclosure from an individual who is otherwise authorized to access protected health information at a facility operated by a covered entity or a business associate to another similar situated individual at the same facility; and
- Any such information received as a result of such disclosure is not further acquired, accessed, used or disclosed without authorization by any person.

Source: ARRA, Section 13400(1).

As discussed in chapter 2, that definition was modified somewhat in the August 2009 HHS breach notification regulations. The modified definition appears in figure 6.2.

**Figure 6.2.   Definition of breach from 45 CFR Part 164, Section 164.402**

*Breach* means the acquisition, access, use, or disclosure of protected health information in a manner not permitted under subpart E of this part which compromises the security or privacy of the protected health information (PHI).

(1)(i) For purposes of this definition, *compromises the security or privacy of the protected health information* means poses a significant risk of financial, reputational, or other harm to the individual.

Unresolved Questions and Conflicts 57

(ii) A use or disclosure of protected health information that does not include the identifiers listed at section 164.514(e)(2), date of birth, and zip code does not compromise the security of the protected health information.

(2) Breach excludes:

(i) Any unintentional acquisition, access, or use of protected health information by a workforce member or person acting under the authority of a covered entity or a business associate, if such acquisition, access, or use was made in good faith and within the scope of authority and does not result in further use of disclosure in a manner not permitted under subpart E of this part.

(ii) Any inadvertent disclosure by a person who is authorized to access protected health information at a covered entity or business associate to another person authorized to access protected health information at the same covered entity or business associate, or organized health care arrangement in which the covered entity participates, and the information received as a result of such disclosure is not further used or disclosed in a manner not permitted under subpart E of this part.

(iii) A disclosure of protected health information where a covered entity or business associate has a good faith belief that an unauthorized person to whom the disclosure was made would not reasonably have been able to retain such information.

---

The two definitions have some subtle differences, but the regulatory "clarification" will be the definition that covered entities will use in building their own policies. And that definition has two basic conditions that must be met for an event to be considered a "breach."

- There must be an acquisition, access, use, or disclosure that is not permitted by the Privacy Rule; and

- That acquisition, access, use or disclosure must compromise the security or privacy of the PHI—in other words, that poses a significant risk of financial, reputational, or other harm to the individual.

Therefore, just because some acquisition, access, use of disclosure violates the privacy rule does not mean it is automatically considered a breach, triggering the notification process. It must also compromise the security or privacy of the information. And, one must take into account whether there is a "significant" risk of financial, reputation, or other harm to the individual. In addition, even if there is an unauthorized acquisition, access, use, or disclosure, it is not considered a breach if that acquisition, access, or use of disclosure does not violate the Privacy Rule.

Here's an example: visitors walking down the hall of a nursing facility overhear staff talking quietly in a staff office. Staff are discussing a patient by name. Is it an unauthorized acquisition, access, use or disclosure? Yes; it's an unauthorized disclosure to the visitor. Does it compromise the security or privacy of the information? That depends on the analysis of whether there's a significant risk of harm, but for this example, assume it compromises the security of privacy of the information. But does the disclosure made by the staff violate the Privacy Rule? No; the circumstances probably qualify this as an "incidental" disclosure under the Privacy Rule. So, one of the main conditions for a breach is not met, and this event would not be considered a breach under the law.

Another common question will be about how much risk must be present to be considered "significant"? The law is silent and leaves the covered entity and business associate to use judgment in analyzing the event, but the regulations do require the risk assessment to factor in the financial, reputation, and other risks.

## Breach Exceptions

As noted in figure 6.2, there are three exceptions to the definition of breach:

**Exception 1** covers any *unintentional* acquisition, access, or use of protected health information by a workforce member or person acting under the authority of a covered entity or business associate if:

- Such acquisition, access, or use was made in *good faith* and within the scope of authority, and
- Does not result in further use of disclosure in a manner not permitted under subpart E of this part.

An example would be a physical therapist who, as part of her job, uses the hospital EHR to look up some information for a patient named Mary Jones, whom this employee has been asked to treat. Unfortunately, the hospital is currently treating two Mary Jones—Mary A. Jones and Mary B. Jones, and the physical therapist accesses the PHI for the wrong patient. Was she authorized to see that Mary Jones' information? No. Could this pose a significant risk to the PHI? During a risk analysis, it is revealed that the employee and the Mary Jones whose information was accessed happen to know each other socially; so there is a significant reputational risk. However, look at the exception: this was an *unintentional* access and was clearly done while acting under her authority as a physical therapist asking to see a patient. She was acting in good faith, and she is normally allowed to access her patients' information. Therefore, assuming she does not further use or disclose the information in a way not permitted by the Privacy Rule, for example, gossiping to family or friends about what she saw, exception 1 applies and this would not be considered a breach.

**Exception 2** covers any *inadvertent* disclosure by a person who is authorized to access PHI at a covered entity or a business associate to another person authorized to access PHI at the same covered entity (CE) or business associate (BA), or organized healthcare arrangement in which the CE participates; *and* the information received as a result of such disclosure is not further used or disclosed in a manner not permitted under subpart E of this part.

# Unresolved Questions and Conflicts

An example of that could be as follows: while collecting paper medical records off the nursing units for discharged patients as part of his normal job, a hospital courier accidentally drops some pages of a patients' record in the hallway. They are picked up by a nurse, who glances at it and returns it to the courier. In this case, both the courier and nurse were authorized to access PHI, the disclosure was inadvertent, and the information was not further used or disclosed, so exception 2 applies and this is not a breach. However, if the nurse shared details of the dropped report with a friend in the Materials Management department who was not authorized to have access to PHI, the exception would not apply.

**Exception 3** covers a disclosure of PHI where a CE and BA has a *good faith belief* that an unauthorized person to whom the disclosure was made would not reasonably have been able to retain such information. As noted in chapter 2, an example of this would be where Explanation of Benefits (EOB) letters were sent to the wrong patients, but were returned by the post office as undeliverable and were unopened.

Even with these simple examples, the language used in the law and the variety of conditions and exceptions that must be considered will make the process of defining a breach rather difficult—especially at first. Watch for official guidance and advice on the meaning of phrases such as "reasonably have been able to retain," "good faith," and "similarly situated individual." In the meantime, it could be very useful to document one's analyses of potential breaches using some sort of checklist or decision tree, populated by the clauses within the Act. At the very least, this can show a reasonable attempt to adhere to the law, even if one's interpretation proves to be flawed.

## Business Associate Agreements

Another as-yet unresolved issue is whether ARRA requires business associate agreements to explicitly include their new privacy- and security-related obligations under the law. This would require amending most existing business associate agreements that currently exist.

Section 13401 states that "Sections 184.308, 164.310, 164.312, and 164.316 of Title 45, Code of Federal Regulations (referring to parts of the Privacy Rule), shall apply to a business associate of a covered entity in the same manner that such sections apply to the covered entity. The additional requirements of this title that relate to security and that are made applicable with respect to covered entities shall also be applicable to such a business associate *and shall be incorporated into the business associate agreement between the business associate and the covered entity*" [emphasis added] (ARRA Section 13401(a)). The question is whether incorporation requires explicit mention, or whether that can be by operation of law (by the Act requiring it to be applicable), or in the alternative, whether agreements containing a generic statement such as "the business associate is required to comply with all present and future applicable privacy- and security-related laws and regulations during the term of the agreement" would suffice.

Some law firms have addressed this question in their client newsletters, and at present, the advice varies. Until this issue is settled definitively, be sure to involve legal counsel in determining the best strategy.

Helpful guidance could come from many sources, not just official guidance from HHS. There are a number of organizations engaged in policy efforts related to privacy and security of health information, and these may also be helpful resources while implementing the provisions of ARRA. Chapter 7 examines some of these efforts and organizations.

## References

American Recovery and Reinvestment Act of 2009. Public Law 111-5.

Department of Health and Human Services. 2009 (August 24). Interim final rule: Breach notification for unsecured protected health information. *Federal Register*. Washington, DC: Government Printing Office.

Family Educational Rights and Privacy Act of 1974 (20 USC 1232g; 34 CFR 99).

42 CFR Part 2. Confidentiality of Alcohol and Drug Abuse Patient Records. 1975.

# Chapter 7

# Policy Efforts Impacting the Privacy Rules of ARRA

A number of national groups and organizations are having a substantial influence on U.S. health information privacy policy. This chapter offers a brief overview of some of these groups' work and also includes the Nationwide Privacy and Security Framework issued by the Office of the National Coordinator for Health IT. Understanding the framework, as well as the work product of the groups listed here, sheds light on what the near-term future may hold for U.S. health information privacy policy.

In addition to the resources and work discussed here, the CD-ROM accompanying this book lists a number of useful Web-based resources on health information privacy and security in appendix B.

## The Nationwide Privacy and Security Framework

The principles of the Nationwide Privacy and Security Framework for Electronic Exchange of Individually Identifiable Health Information, listed in figure 7.1, seeks to establish a single, consistent approach to address the privacy and security challenges related to electronic health information exchange through a network for all persons, regardless of the legal framework that may apply to a particular organization. The goal of this effort was to establish a policy framework for electronic health information exchange that can help guide the nation's adoption of health information technologies and help improve the availability of health information and therefore improve healthcare quality. The principles, boldfaced in the figure, have been designed to establish the roles of individuals who are the subject of health information and the responsibilities of those parties who hold and exchange electronic individually identifiable health information through a network. The framework was issued in December 2008. Figure 7.1 includes not only the principles themselves, but an excellent overview of the history of the government's work on the issues of privacy and security, and includes references for those who like to know more about not only U.S. history on the subject, but also the approach of other countries.

## Figure 7.1. Nationwide Privacy and Security Framework for Electronic Exchange of Individually Identifiable Health Information

### I. Preamble

**PURPOSE**

Electronic health information exchange promises an array of potential benefits for individuals and the U.S. health care system through improved clinical care and reduced cost. At the same time, this environment also poses new challenges and opportunities for protecting individually identifiable health information. In health care, accurate and complete information about individuals is critical to providing high quality, coordinated care. If individuals and other participants in a network lack trust in electronic exchange of information due to perceived or actual risks to individually identifiable health information or the accuracy and completeness of such information, it may affect their willingness to disclose necessary health information and could have life-threatening consequences. A key factor to achieving a high-level of trust among individuals, health care providers, and other health care organizations participating in electronic health information exchange is the development of, and adherence to, a consistent and coordinated approach to privacy and security. Clear, understandable, uniform principles are a first step in developing a consistent and coordinated approach to privacy and security and a key component to building the trust required to realize the potential benefits of electronic health information exchange.

The principles below establish a single, consistent approach to address the privacy and security challenges related to electronic health information exchange through a network for all persons, regardless of the legal framework that may apply to a particular organization. The goal of this effort is to establish a policy framework for electronic health information exchange that can help guide the Nation's adoption of health information technologies and help improve the availability of health information and health care quality. The principles have been designed to establish the roles of individuals and the responsibilities of those who hold and exchange electronic individually identifiable health information through a network.

**BACKGROUND**

Numerous forces are driving the health care industry towards the use of health information technology, such as the potential for reducing medical errors and health care costs, and increasing individuals' involvement in their own health and health care. To facilitate this advancement and reap its benefits while reducing the risks, it is important to consider individual privacy interests together with the potential benefits to population health.

**Historical Perspective**

The Federal government has long recognized the importance of privacy and security protections for the electronic collection, use, and disclosure of individually identifiable information and principles or practices to guide those actions. As early as 1973, the U.S. Department of Health, Education, and Welfare (HEW) appointed the Advisory Committee on Automated Personal

Data Systems to analyze the consequences of using computers to keep records about people. In order to benefit from computerization while providing privacy safeguards, the advisory committee developed the *Code of Fair Information Practice*, which addresses five practices: openness, disclosure, secondary use, correction, and security. These practices have influenced many U.S. laws at both the Federal and state levels and also numerous other national and international documents. For example, in 1974, the Privacy Act was passed, which protects certain personal information held by Federal agencies. In 1980, the Organisation for Economic Cooperation and Development (OECD), an international organization comprised of 24 countries including the U.S., published a consensus document, the *Guidelines on the Protection of Privacy and Transborder Flows of Personal Data*. The purpose of the Guidelines was to decrease disparities and assist in harmonizing legislation that would allow the flow of data while preventing violations of what the OECD member countries considered fundamental human rights. In 1998, the Federal Trade Commission published *Privacy Online: a Report to Congress,* which among other conclusions stated that effective self-regulation is the preferred approach to protecting individuals' privacy. Most recently, the U.S. Department of Health and Human Services (HHS) built on these principles in developing the Privacy Rule under the Health Insurance Portability and Accountability Act of 1996 (HIPAA).

In 2004, the Office of the National Coordinator for Health Information Technology (ONC) was created by E.O. 13335, which charged the National Coordinator to the extent permitted by law, to develop, maintain, and direct the implementation of, a strategic plan to guide the nationwide implementation of interoperable health information technology in both the public and private health care sectors and to address in the plan, among other things, "privacy and security issues related to interoperable health information technology and recommend methods to ensure appropriate authorization, authentication, and encryption of data for transmission over the Internet…."

**Legal Environment**

Over several decades, states have passed laws to protect the privacy of health information. These laws differ from state to state and often narrowly target a particular population, health condition, data collection effort, or specific types of health care organizations. As a result, states have created a patchwork of privacy protections that are not comprehensive or easily understood. Many states also have begun to consider information security related issues and have passed laws, for example, requiring various types of entities to provide notice of security breaches of individually identifiable information.

At the Federal level, there are also a variety of laws related to the privacy and security of health information, including the HIPAA Privacy and Security Rules, the Privacy Act of 1974, the Confidentiality of Alcohol and Drug Abuse Patient Records Regulation (42 CFR Part 2), the Family Educational Rights & Privacy Act (addresses privacy of information held by certain educational institutions), Gramm-Leach-Bliley Financial Services Act (addresses privacy of information held by financial institutions), and Federal Information Security Management Act of 2002 (FISMA).

**Figure 7.1. Nationwide Privacy and Security Framework for Electronic Exchange of Individually Identifiable Health Information** *(continued)*

The Privacy and Security Rules promulgated under HIPAA were the first Federal regulations to broadly address the privacy and security of health information. They establish a baseline of national privacy and security standards for individually identifiable health information held by "covered entities" and a foundation of protection regardless of health condition, type of health program, population, state where the activity occurs, or other situational characteristics.

Although the HIPAA Privacy and Security Rules apply to health information in electronic form, the current landscape of electronic health information exchange poses new issues and involves additional organizations that were not contemplated at the time the rules were drafted.

## METHODOLOGY

In the development of the Nationwide Privacy and Security Framework for Electronic Exchange of Individually Identifiable Health Information, ONC reviewed various international, national, and public and private sector privacy and security principles that focused on individual information in an electronic environment (but not necessarily on health), including those that focused on individually identifiable health information. This review included:

- *HEW Advisory Committee's Code of Fair Information Practice[i]*

- Markle Foundation's *Connecting Consumers: Common Framework for Networked Personal Health Information[ii]*

- Organisation for Economic Co-operation and Development (OECD) *Guidelines on the Protection of Privacy and Transborder Flows of Personal Data[iii]*

- *Health Information Technology—Consumer Principles[iv]*

- Federal Trade Commission's *Privacy Online: A Report to Congress—Fair Information Practice Principles[v]*

- The International Security Trust and Privacy Alliance's (ISTPA): *Privacy Framework[vi]* It is worth noting that ISTPA conducted a privacy and security principles analysis and harmonization, while accommodating variation from the following instruments, which resulted in the ISTPA principles reviewed by HHS.

- *Privacy Act of 1974*

- OECD *Guidelines on the Protection of Privacy and Transborder Flows of Personal Data*

- UN Guidelines Concerning Personalized Computer Files

- EU Data Protection Directive 95/46/EC

- Canadian Standards Association Model Code (incorporated in the Personal Information Protection and Electronic Documents Act [PIPEDA])

- *Health Insurance Portability and Accountability Act of 1996 (HIPAA)* Privacy Rules
- U.S. FTC Statement of Fair Information Practice Principles
- U.S.-E.U. Safe Harbor Privacy Principles
- Australian Privacy Act—National Privacy Principles
- Japan Personal Information Protection Act
- APEC (Asia-Pacific Economic Cooperation) Privacy Framework

There was a great deal of commonality across these principles. After a careful review and analysis of these principles, we harmonized them while accommodating as much variation as possible and being careful to consider how they may apply to electronic health information exchange. We also reviewed the approaches taken by various Federal laws, specifically the HIPAA Privacy and Security Rules, the Privacy Act, and FISMA, as well as recommendations that the Secretary had approved from two advisory committees, the National Committee on Vital and Health Statistics (NCVHS) and the American Health Information Community (AHIC).

## PRINCIPLES

The principles outlined in the Nationwide Privacy and Security Framework for Electronic Exchange of Individually Identifiable Health Information serve as a guide for public and private-sector entities that hold or exchange electronic individually identifiable health information and the development of any compliance and enforcement approaches, including industry self-regulation. Additionally, these principles are designed to complement and work with existing Federal, state, territorial, local, and tribal laws and regulations and should not be construed or interpreted as supplanting or altering any applicable laws or regulations. Various Federal Government agencies are expected to look to these principles as the framework for their policy and technology activities in this area and to encourage states and private sector organizations to do the same.

The implementation of these principles should be dynamic and subject to modification as information practices and technologies advance; however, these principles are designed to be applicable as technology changes.

### Scope

*These principles are expected to guide the actions of all health care-related persons and entities that participate in a network for the purpose of electronic exchange of individually identifiable health information. These principles are not intended to apply to individuals with respect to their own individually identifiable health information.*

By adopting these principles, persons and entities will follow a common approach to privacy and security and develop appropriate and comparable protections for information, thereby increasing trust in electronic exchange of individually identifiable health information. These principles do not apply to individuals with respect to their own individually identifiable health informa-

**Figure 7.1. Nationwide Privacy and Security Framework for Electronic Exchange of Individually Identifiable Health Information** *(continued)*

tion. Individuals may use and/or disclose their individual health information as they choose. For example, an individual may share details of a chronic disease on the Internet or in a public meeting but may decide not to share that information with all his or her health care providers or employers. Likewise, an individual should not be expected to implement the administrative responsibilities of these principles such as developing policies and procedures.

**Organization of the Principles**

The framework is comprised of eight principles that are organized as follows:

- Principles (Level I): Each principle is made up of a short title and a concise statement designed to clearly and simply reflect the concept embodied within each: Individual Access; Correction; Openness and Transparency; Individual Choice; Collection, Use, and Disclosure Limitation; Data Quality and Integrity; Safeguards; and Accountability.

- Detail (Level II): Each principle is followed by a short explanation that further elaborates on the principle, what it is designed to do, and its parameters.

**Terminology**

In order to best understand the scope and application of the principles, it is recommended that the reader refer to the glossary (Appendix 1), particularly with respect to the definitions of "individuals" and "persons and entities."

**II. The Nationwide Privacy and Security Framework for Electronic Exchange of Individually Identifiable Health Information**

*SCOPE*

*These principles are expected to guide the actions of all health care-related persons and entities that participate in a network for the purpose of electronic exchange of individually identifiable health information. These principles are not intended to apply to individuals with respect to their own individually identifiable health information.*

*INTRODUCTION*

Adoption of privacy and security protections are essential to establishing the public trust necessary for effective electronic exchange of individually identifiable health information. A common set of principles that stakeholders accept and support is the first step towards realizing those privacy and security protections and establishing the necessary public trust. The approach of developing principles to guide information practices while advancing technology was marked by the 1973 release of the Code of Fair Information Practice and has been the basis for various activities in the public and private sectors, including the development of the Health Insurance Portability and Accountability Act (HIPAA) Privacy Rule and as the basis for this framework.

The implementation of these principles should evolve in concert with technological advances that allow for greater protections. Adherence should be the responsibility of each health care-related person or entity that holds and exchanges electronic individually identifiable health information through a network, as well as the responsibility of other persons and entities that receive or have access to such information, so that electronic individually identifiable health information is protected at all times.

These principles do not constitute legal advice and do not affect a person's or entity's duty to comply with applicable legal requirements. Where these principles set higher standards than legal requirements, adherence to these principles is encouraged.

## INDIVIDUAL ACCESS

Individuals should be provided with a simple and timely means to access and obtain their individually identifiable health information in a readable form and format.

*Access to information enables individuals to manage their health care and well-being. Individuals should have a reasonable means of access to their individually identifiable health information. Individuals should be able to obtain this information easily, consistent with security needs for authentication of the individual; and such information should be provided promptly so as to be useful for managing their health. Additionally, the persons and entities, that participate in a network for the purpose of electronic exchange of individually identifiable health information, should provide such information in a readable form and format, including an electronic format, when appropriate. In limited instances, medical or other circumstances may result in the appropriate denial of individual access to their health information.*

## CORRECTION

Individuals should be provided with a timely means to dispute the accuracy or integrity of their individually identifiable health information, and to have erroneous information corrected or to have a dispute documented if their requests are denied.

*Individuals have an important stake in the accuracy and integrity of their individually identifiable health information and an important role to play in ensuring its accuracy and integrity. Electronic exchange of individually identifiable health information may improve care and reduce adverse events. However, any errors or conclusions drawn from erroneous data may be easily communicated or replicated (e.g., as a result of an administrative error as simple as a transposed digit or more complex error arising from medical identity theft). For this reason it is essential for individuals to have practical, efficient, and timely means for disputing the accuracy or integrity of their individually identifiable health information, to have this information corrected, or a dispute documented when their requests are denied, and to have the correction or dispute communicated to others with whom the underlying information has been shared. Persons and entities, that participate in a network for the purpose of electronic exchange of individually identifiable health information, should make processes available to empower individuals to exercise a role in managing their individually identifiable health information and should correct information or document disputes in a timely fashion.*

**Figure 7.1. Nationwide Privacy and Security Framework for Electronic Exchange of Individually Identifiable Health Information** *(continued)*

### OPENNESS AND TRANSPARENCY

There should be openness and transparency about policies, procedures, and technologies that directly affect individuals and/or their individually identifiable health information.

*Trust in electronic exchange of individually identifiable health information can best be established in an open and transparent environment. Individuals should be able to understand what individually identifiable health information exists about them, how that individually identifiable health information is collected, used, and disclosed and whether and how they can exercise choice over such collections, uses, and disclosures. Persons and entities, that participate in a network for the purpose of electronic exchange of individually identifiable health information, should provide reasonable opportunities for individuals to review who has accessed their individually identifiable health information or to whom it has been disclosed, in a readable form and format. Notice of policies, procedures, and technology—including what information will be provided under what circumstances—should be timely and, wherever possible, made in advance of the collection, use, and/or disclosure of individually identifiable health information. Policies and procedures developed consistent with this* Nationwide Privacy and Security Framework for Electronic Exchange of Individually Identifiable Health Information *should be communicated in a manner that is appropriate and understandable to individuals.*

### INDIVIDUAL CHOICE

Individuals should be provided a reasonable opportunity and capability to make informed decisions about the collection, use, and disclosure of their individually identifiable health information.

*The ability of individuals to make choices with respect to electronic exchange of individually identifiable health information concerning them is important to building trust. Persons and entities, that participate in a network for the purpose of electronic exchange of individually identifiable health information, should provide reasonable opportunities and capabilities for individuals to exercise choice with respect to their individually identifiable health information. The degree of choice made available may vary with the type of information being exchanged, the purpose of the exchange, and the recipient of the information. Applicable law, population health needs, medical necessity, ethical principles, and technology, among other factors, may affect options for expressing choice. Individuals should be able to designate someone else, such as a family member, care-giver, or legal guardian, to make decisions on their behalf. When an individual exercises choice, including the ability to designate someone else to make decisions on his or her behalf, the process should be fair and not unduly burdensome.*

### COLLECTION, USE, AND DISCLOSURE LIMITATION

Individually identifiable health information should be collected, used, and/or disclosed only to the extent necessary to accomplish a specified purpose(s) and never to discriminate inappropriately.

*Establishing appropriate limits on the type and amount of information collected, used, and/or disclosed increases privacy protections and is essential to building trust in* electronic exchange of individually identifiable health information because it minimizes potential misuse and abuse. Persons and entities that participate in a network for the purpose of electronic exchange *of individually identifiable health information, should only collect, use, and/or disclose information necessary to accomplish a specified purpose(s). Persons and entities should take advantage of technological advances to limit data collection, use, and/or disclosure.*

## DATA QUALITY AND INTEGRITY

Persons and entities should take reasonable steps to ensure that individually identifiable health information is complete, accurate, and up-to-date to the extent necessary for the person's or entity's intended purposes and has not been altered or destroyed in an unauthorized manner.

*The completeness and accuracy of an individual's health information may affect, among other things, the quality of care that the individual receives, medical decisions, and health outcomes.* Persons and entities, that participate in a network for the purpose of electronic exchange of individually identifiable health information, have a responsibility to maintain individually identifiable health information that is useful for its intended purposes, which involves taking reasonable steps to ensure that information is accurate, complete, and up-to-date, and has not been altered or destroyed in an unauthorized manner. Persons and entities have a responsibility to update or correct individually identifiable health information and to provide timely notice of these changes to others with whom the underlying information has been shared. Moreover, persons and entities should develop processes to detect, prevent, and mitigate any unauthorized changes to, or deletions of, individually identifiable health information.

## SAFEGUARDS

Individually identifiable health information should be protected with reasonable administrative, technical, and physical safeguards to ensure its confidentiality, integrity, and availability and to prevent unauthorized or inappropriate access, use, or disclosure.

*Trust in electronic exchange of individually identifiable health information can only be achieved if reasonable administrative, technical, and physical safeguards are in place to protect individually identifiable health information and minimize the risks of unauthorized or inappropriate access, use, or disclosure. These safeguards should be developed after a thorough assessment to determine any risks or vulnerabilities to individually identifiable health information. Persons and entities, that participate in a network for the purpose of electronic exchange of individually identifiable health information, should implement administrative, technical, and physical safeguards to protect information, including assuring that only authorized persons and entities and employees of such persons or entities have access to individually identifiable health information. Administrative, technical, and physical safeguards should be reasonable in scope and balanced with the need for access to individually identifiable health information.*

**Figure 7.1. Nationwide Privacy and Security Framework for Electronic Exchange of Individually Identifiable Health Information** *(continued)*

## ACCOUNTABILITY

These principles should be implemented, and adherence assured, through appropriate monitoring, and other means and methods should be in place to report and mitigate non-adherence and breaches.

*These nationwide privacy and security principles will not be effective in building trust in electronic exchange of individually identifiable health information unless there is compliance with these Principles and enforcement mechanisms. Mechanisms for assuring accountability include policies and procedures and other tools. At a minimum, such mechanisms adopted by persons and entities, that participate in a network for the purpose of electronic exchange of individually identifiable health information, should address: (1) monitoring for internal compliance including authentication and authorizations for access to or disclosure of individually identifiable health information; (2) the ability to receive and act on complaints, including taking corrective measures; and (3) the provision of reasonable mitigation measures, including notice to individuals of privacy violations or security breaches that pose substantial risk of harm to such individuals.*

i The U.S. Department of Health, Education and Welfare now the U.S. Department of Health and Human Services: http://www.hhs.gov/ *Report of the Secretary's Advisory Committee on Automated Personal Data Systems* (1973): http://aspe.hhs.gov/DATACNCL/1973privacy/tocprefacemembers.htm

ii Markle Foundation: http://www.markle.org/ *Common Framework for Networked Personal Health Information: Overview and Principles (Current as of 2008)*: http://www.connectingforhealth.org/phti/reports/overview.html

iii Organisation for Economic Co-operation and Development (OECD): http://www.oecd.org/home/0,2987,en_2649_201185_1_1_1_1_1,00.html *Guidelines on the Protection of Privacy and Transborder Flows of Personal Data (1980):* http://www.oecd.org/document/18/0,3343,en_2649_34255_1815186_1_1_1_1,00.html

iv H*ealth Information Technology—Consumer Principles* (2006), Endorsed by: AARP; AFL-CIO; American Federation of State, County and Municipal Employees; American Federation of Teachers; Center for Medical Consumers; Communications Workers of America; Consumers Union; Department for Professional Employees, AFL-CIO; Childbirth Connection; Health Care for All; Health Privacy Project; International Association of Machinists and Aerospace Workers; International Union, United Auto Workers; National Coalition for Cancer Survivorship; National Consumers League; National Partnership for Women and Families; Service Employees International Union; Title II Community AIDS National Network; United Steelworkers International Union (USW): http://www.nclnet.org/health/final%202006%20principles%20PDF.pdf

v Federal Trade Commission (FTC): http://www.ftc.gov/. Privacy Online: A Report to Congress (1998) – Fair Information Practice Principles: http://www.ftc.gov/reports/privacy3/fairinfo.shtm

vi International Security Trust and Privacy Alliance (ISTPA): www.istpa.org. Analysis of Privacy Principles: An Operational Study (2007, Version 1.8): http://www.istpa.org/pdfs/ISTPAAnalysisofPrivacyPrinciplesV2.pdf

## GLOSSARY

**Administrative safeguards:** Administrative actions, and policies and procedures to manage the selection, development, implementation, and maintenance of security measures to protect electronic individually identifiable health information and to manage the conduct of the entity's workforce in relation to the protection of that information. Administrative safeguards include policies and procedures, workforce training, risk management plans, and contingency plans.

**Collect/Collection:** The acquisition or receipt of information, including individually identifiable health information.

**Corrective Measures:** Actions taken to address a security breach or privacy violation, with the intent to counteract the breach or violation and reduce future risks.

**Disclose/Disclosure:** The release, transfer, exchange, provision of access to, or divulging in any other manner of information outside the person or entity holding the information.

**Health Information:** Any information that relates to the past, present, or future physical or mental health or condition of an individual; the provision of health care to an individual; or the past, present, or future payment for the provision of health care to an individual.

**Individual:** A person who is the recipient of health and/or wellness services.

**Individually Identifiable Health Information:** Health information that identifies the individual, or with respect to which there is a reasonable basis to believe the information can be used to identify the individual.

**Open:** Actively communicating information through notice or otherwise.

**Persons and Entities:** Health care professionals, partnerships, proprietorships, corporations, and other types of organizations and their agents when acting on their behalf.

**Physical Safeguards:** Physical measures, policies and procedures to protect electronic information systems and related buildings and equipment from natural and environmental hazards and unauthorized intrusion. Physical safeguards include workstation security and use procedures, facility security plans, data backup and storage, and portable device and media controls.

**Privacy:** An individual's interest in protecting his or her individually identifiable health information and the corresponding obligation of those persons and entities that participate in a network for the purposes of electronic exchange of such information, to respect those interests through fair information practices.

**Security:** The physical, technological, and administrative safeguards used to protect individually identifiable health information.

**Technical Safeguards:** The technology and the policies and procedures for its use that protect electronic individually identifiable health information and control access to it.

**Transparent:** Making information readily and publicly available.

**Use:** Is the employment, application, utilization, examination, analysis or maintenance of individually identifiable health information.

Source: HHS, 2008.

## **Growing Role of the Federal Trade Commission**

Chapter 5 introduces the concept of a growing role for the Federal Trade Commission (FTC) in health information privacy and security. Privacy is a central element of the FTC's consumer protection mission. But their consumer-directed materials and Web site express concern about how advances in computer technology have made it possible for detailed information about people to be compiled and shared more easily and cheaply than ever. The FTC acknowledges that this has produced many benefits for society as a whole, and for individual consumers. But their materials warn that, at the same time, as personal information becomes more accessible, everyone—companies, associations, government agencies, and consumers—must take precautions to protect against the misuse of information.

The following sections discuss several resources and activities of the FTC on point, to show the current priorities of both their enforcement and policy-making activities, beyond the CVS Caremark action already described in chapter 5.

On April 16, 2009, the FTC published a *Federal Register* notice seeking public comment on a proposed rule that would require certain organizations (other than covered entities and organizations acting as business associates) to notify consumers when the security of their electronic PHR health information is breached. After receiving comment, the FTC issued a final Health Breach Notification Rule on August 25, 2009. As discussed briefly in chapter 2, ARRA includes provisions to advance the use of health information technology and, at the same time, strengthen privacy and security protections for health information. ARRA recognizes that there are new types of Web-based entities that collect or handle consumers' sensitive health information. Some of these entities offer personal health records (PHRs) that consumers can use as an electronic, individually controlled repository for their medical information. Others provide online applications through which consumers can track and manage different kinds of information in their personal health records (PHRs). Others may simply be companies that have nothing to do with healthcare, but lease server space to PHR vendors and therefore may have access to PHR information. The FTC announcement cited the example of a device such as a pedometer that can upload miles traveled, heart rate, and other data into their personal health records through the consumer's computer. The FTC noted that these innovations have the potential to provide numerous benefits for consumers, which can only be realized if they have confidence that the security and confidentiality of their health information will be maintained.

To address these issues, ARRA requires HHS to conduct a study and report, in consultation with the FTC, on potential privacy, security, and breach notification requirements for PHR vendors and related entities. This study and report must be completed by February 2010. In the interim, the Act requires the Commission to issue a temporary rule requiring these entities to notify consumers if the security of their health information is breached. The rule issued on August 25, 2009, is the first step in implementing this requirement.

In keeping with ARRA, the rule requires vendors of PHRs and related entities to provide notice to consumers following a breach of security. The rule also stipulates that if a service provider to

Policy Efforts Impacting the Privacy Rules of ARRA

one of these entities experiences a breach, it must notify the entity, which in turn must notify consumers of the breach. The rule contains additional requirements governing the standard for what triggers the notice, as well as the timing, method, and content of notice. It also requires entities covered by the rule to notify the FTC of any breaches. The FTC can then post information about the breaches on its Web site, and must notify the HHS Secretary.

The FTC has also been active on the subject of medical identity theft. On October 15, 2008, the FTC worked with ONC to host a Town Hall meeting on medical identity theft that focused on how medical identity theft should be addressed in a health information technology (IT) environment and was attended by stakeholders from the public and private sectors. The FTC's interest in medical identity theft is also part of a larger focus on identity theft in general. The "red flag" program required by the FTC to ensure that systems are in place to prevent and detect identity theft in certain organizations was made applicable to almost all healthcare providers as well, as explained in figure 7.2. This figure is a letter the FTC wrote to the American Medical Association (AMA) explaining their position on the applicability of the red flag rules to providers.

## ONC's HIT Policy Committee

The Health IT Policy Committee's charge is to make recommendations to the National Coordinator for Health Information Technology (HIT) on a policy framework for the development and adoption of a nationwide health information infrastructure, including standards for the exchange of patient health information. Formation of the committee was a requirement of ARRA. Section 3002 of ARRA provides that the HIT Policy Committee shall at least make recommendations on standards, implementation specifications, and certifications criteria in eight specific areas. Those areas include:

- The electronic exchange and use of health information and the enterprise integration of such information

- The utilization of an EHR for each person in the United States by 2014

- The incorporation of privacy and security protections for the electronic exchange of an individual's individually identifiable health information

- Ensuring security methods to provide for appropriate authorization and electronic authentication of health information and specifying technologies or methodologies for rendering health information unusable, unreadable, or indecipherable

- Specifying a framework for coordination and flow of recommendations and policies under this subtitle among the Secretary, the National Coordinator, the HIT Policy Committee, the HIT Standards Committee, and other health information exchanges and other relevant entities

## Figure 7.2. FTC letter to the American Medical Association on red flag applicability

UNITED STATES OF AMERICA
FEDERAL TRADE COMMISSION
WASHINGTON, D.C. 20580

Office of the Director
Bureau of Consumer Protection

February 4, 2009

Ms. Margaret Garikes
Director of Federal Affairs, American Medical Association
25 Massachusetts Ave., N.W., Suite 600
Washington, D.C. 20001

Dear Ms. Garikes:

    I am writing in response to your correspondence in which the American Medical Association ("AMA") along with other medical associations challenge the position taken by the staff of the Federal Trade Commission ("FTC" or "Commission") regarding the applicability of the Identity Theft Red Flags Rule ("Red Flags Rule" or "Rule")[1] to physicians and related health care providers. In your letter, you assert that medical care providers are not covered by the Rule because they are not "creditors" as that term is defined in the law. In discussions with staff you also have suggested that even if health care providers were considered creditors in some circumstances, they should not be required to comply with the Rule because they already comply with regulations under the Health Insurance Portability and Accountability Act ("HIPAA"). And finally, you have expressed concern that application of the Red Flags Rule to health care providers could have unintended consequences on the practice of medicine.

    After we received your initial letter, FTC staff arranged to meet with your staff and representatives from other health care provider organizations on November 19, 2008, to discuss the concerns raised in your letter. We found the meeting and the interchange of ideas informative and helpful, and came away with a greater understanding of your position and the manner in which health care professionals handle payment and credit issues. We welcome further dialogue, and believe that we can achieve an outcome that does not place undue or unnecessary burdens on health care professionals, but still meets the desired goal of the Rule to reduce the overall incidence and impact of identity theft, including medical identity theft.

    As staff has discussed with you, we believe that the plain language and purpose of the Rule dictate that health care professionals are covered by the Rule when they regularly defer payment for goods or services. We also believe that implementation of the Rule will help reduce the incidence of medical identity theft; and that the burden on health care professionals need not be substantial. This letter will address each of these points.

---

[1] 16 C.F.R. § 681.1 (2007).

## Background of the Red Flags Rule

In part to respond to the disturbing increase in identity theft, Congress passed the Fair and Accurate Credit Transactions Act of 2003 ("FACTA"),[2] amending the Fair Credit Reporting Act ("FCRA").[3] Among the many provisions in FACTA was a mandate that the FTC, the Federal bank regulatory agencies, and the National Credit Union Administration (the "Agencies") jointly develop rules and guidelines for "financial institutions" and "creditors," both defined terms under the FCRA, regarding identity theft.[4]

Briefly put, the Red Flags Rule requires creditors and financial institutions ("covered entities") to conduct a risk assessment to determine if they have "covered accounts," which include consumer-type accounts or other accounts for which there is a reasonable risk of identity theft. If so, the covered entity must develop and implement a written Identity Theft Program ("Program") to identify, detect, and respond to possible risks of identity theft relevant to them. Such risks could include, for example, whether the manner in which accounts are opened could make them more susceptible to the perpetration of fraud, the entity's earlier experiences with identity theft, or types of suspicious activity relating to the opening of or access to an account. The entities then must specify how they will detect the warning signs – or red flags – that indicate an identity thief may be at work. This process might include examining a consumer's identification document or detecting unusual patterns with respect to use of an account. Finally, the Program must detail how to respond once the entity has detected a red flag. Responses might include refraining from billing the consumer whose identity was misused, ensuring that information relating to the identity thief is not commingled with information relating to the victim (e.g., medical records or consumer reports), or reporting an incident of identity theft to a law enforcement agency.

The Red Flags Rule is intended to address all forms of identity theft, including those involving the provision of health care.[5] Although identity theft most commonly is associated with financial transactions, there are increasing concerns about identity fraud in the context of medical care.[6] Medical identity theft can surface when a patient seeks care using the name or insurance information of another person, which can result in both

---

[2] Pub. L. 108-159.

[3] 15 U.S.C. § 1681 *et seq.*

[4] A proposed rule was issued by the Agencies on July 18, 2006. Following a 60 day comment period and review of the comments received, the Agencies issued a final rule on November 9, 2007.

[5] *See* 72 Fed. Reg. 63718, 63727 (Nov. 9, 2007).

[6] There is no firm consensus on the definition of the term "medical identity theft," but for the purposes of the Red Flags Rule, "medical identity theft" means identity theft committed for the purpose of obtaining medical services. *Id.* at 63727.

**Figure 7.2.    FTC letter to the American Medical Association on red flag applicability** *(continued)*

false billing and the potentially life-threatening corruption of a patient's medical records.[7] A nationwide survey conducted for the FTC found that 4.5% of the 8.3 million victims of identity theft had experienced some form of medical identity theft, including the fraudulent use of their health insurance to obtain medical care or to obtain health insurance in their name.[8] The incidence of medical identity theft may be increasing.[9] The Department of Health and Human Services held a Town Hall meeting on October 15, 2008, to explore further the problem of medical identity theft and how it should be addressed in a health information technology environment.[10]

Given the potentially serious consequences for the health of victims, many physicians already evaluate their identity theft risk and develop, as appropriate, reasonable prevention programs. For example, some health care providers ask for photo identification at patient visits.[11] These steps are consistent with the objectives of the Red Flags Rule.

### The Definition of Creditor

As noted earlier, the Red Flags Rule applies to creditors and financial institutions. It is the term "creditor" that is relevant to the coverage of medical practitioners. The definition of "creditor"[12] in the FCRA refers directly to the definition of "creditor" in the Equal Credit Opportunity Act ("ECOA").[13] The ECOA defines "creditor" as "any person who regularly extends, renews, or continues credit; any person who regularly arranges for the extension, renewal, or continuation of credit; or any assignee of an original creditor who participates in the decision to extend, renew or continue credit."[14] "Credit," in turn, is defined by the ECOA as "the right granted by a creditor to a debtor to defer payment of debt or to incur debts and defer its payment or to purchase property or services and defer

---

[7] World Privacy Forum, *Medical Identity Theft: The Information Crime That Can Kill You*, May 3, 2006 at http://www.worldprivacyforum.org/pdf/wpf_medicalidtheft2006.pdf.

[8] Synovate 2006 Identity Theft Survey Report (November 2007) at http://www.ftc.gov/os/2007/11/SynovateFinalReportIDTheft2006.pdf.

[9] Michelle Andrews, *Thief vs. Patient: When medical identities get stolen, health and wealth are in danger*, U.S. News & World Rep., Mar. 17, 2008, at 48, *available at* 2008 WLNR 4569182.

[10] *See* http://www.hhs.gov/healthit/privacy/identytheft.html.

[11] Vicki Lee Parker, *Doctors' offices try to ward off medical identity theft*, The Raleigh News & Observer, Nov. 10, 2007, at D1, *available at* 2007 WLNR 22251087.

[12] As it does not appear that physicians currently engage in activities that would make them financial institutions under the FCRA, it is not necessary to discuss the definition in this letter.

[13] 15 U.S.C. § 1681a(r)(5).

[14] 15 U.S.C. § 1691a(e). *Accord* 12 C.F.R. § 202.2(l).

payment therefor."[15] The Agencies concluded that the plain language of the statute covered all entities engaged in the provision of credit, as broadly defined by the ECOA, and does not permit industry-based exclusions.

The focus of the Red Flags Rule on credit transactions is a logical one, because it is those types of transactions that identity thieves can most easily exploit. Identity thieves look for opportunities to obtain products or services that do not require payment up-front. The Agencies recognized, however, the potential burden that the Rule could impose on those creditors that had only a small risk of identity theft.[16] Accordingly, the Agencies designed a rule that is risk-based. The Rule, which requires the use of reasonable processes and procedures to detect, prevent, and mitigate identity theft, enables individual entities to structure their programs in ways that are commensurate with their risk; thus, high risk entities would tend to have more elaborate Programs, while low risk entities could have streamlined and less complex Programs. FTC staff expects that entities for which the risks of identity theft are minimal or non-existent will have a very low burden under the Rule.[17]

There is no bright line test however, that can categorically distinguish between high risk entities and low risk entities. Not only is the definition of an ECOA "creditor" activity-based, not industry-based, but so is the distinction between high and low risk entities. Thus, the nature and extent of identity theft risk that a particular industry or entity might face is relevant to the nature of the Red Flags Program it should adopt, but not to whether it is covered by the Rule in the first instance. For example, a small medical practice with a well-known, limited patient base might have a lower risk of identity theft, and thus might adopt a more limited Program than a clinic in a large metropolitan setting that sees a high volume of patients.

In interpreting the ECOA, courts and federal agencies have recognized its broad remedial nature, including the broad scope of the terms "credit" and "creditor."[18] It can be presumed that Congress was aware of these interpretations when incorporating the ECOA's definitional language into the FACT Act.[19] The Board of Governors of the

---

[15] 15 U.S.C. § 1691a(d). Regulation B, which elaborates on the ECOA, defines "credit" in similar terms: "the right granted by a creditor to an applicant to defer payment of a debt, incur debt and defer its payment, or purchase property or services and defer payment therefor." 12 C.F.R. § 202.2(j).

[16] For example, see the FTC burden estimate analysis at 72 Fed. Reg. 63741.

[17] Id. at 63742.

[18] See Brothers v. First Leasing, 724 F.2d 789, 793-94 (9th Cir. 1984); Williams v. AT&T Wireless Servs., 5 F. Supp. 2d 1142, 1147 (W.D. Wash. 1998).

[19] See Dresser Industries, Inc. v. United States, 238 F.3d 603, 614 n.9 (5th Cir. 2001) ("a fundamental principle of statutory construction is 'that Congress is presumed to be aware of judicial interpretations of the law, and that when Congress enacts a new statute incorporating provisions similar to those in prior law, it is assumed to have acted with awareness of judicial interpretations of prior law.'") (citation omitted).

**Figure 7.2.    FTC letter to the American Medical Association on red flag applicability** *(continued)*

Federal Reserve Board ("Federal Reserve Board"), which has the authority to promulgate regulations and interpretations of the ECOA, *see* 15 U.S.C. 1691(b), has confirmed this broad interpretation of these terms. In accordance with its authority to interpret ECOA terms, the Federal Reserve Board promulgated an implementing regulation, known as Regulation B, as well as an Official Staff Commentary to Regulation B, to serve as a guide to compliance with the ECOA. As the agency with governing authority over the statutory scheme, the Federal Reserve Board's interpretations of the ECOA merit substantial deference.[20]

In its Official Staff Commentary to Regulation B, the Federal Reserve Board makes clear that the terms "creditor" and "credit" under the ECOA should be interpreted broadly so as to include all entities that defer payments, even in the normal course of a traditional billing process.[21] As the Official Staff Commentary states, "[i]f a service provider (such as a hospital, doctor, lawyer, or merchant) allows the client or customer to defer the payment of a bill, this deferral of a debt is credit for purposes of the regulation, even though there is no finance charge and no agreement for payment in installments."[22] This interpretation must be granted deference under the *Chevron* principles.[23]

The Federal bank regulatory agencies, including the Federal Reserve Board, recently reaffirmed this interpretation of the term "creditor." In the preamble to the rules under FACTA covering the use of medical information in credit determinations, those agencies explained that "[c]reditors include depository institutions as well as entities that are neither depository institutions nor affiliates of depository institutions, such as independent finance companies, loan brokers, **health care providers**, and automobile dealers." (emphasis added).[24]

Courts and commentators that have considered the Official Staff Commentary to Regulation B also have acknowledged this broad interpretation of the term "creditor." For example, in *Barney v. Holzer Clinic, Ltd.*,[25] the court cited the Official Staff Commentary in recognizing that medical service providers could be ECOA creditors under certain circumstances. Although the court ultimately held that the plaintiff Medicaid recipients did not qualify as "debtors" under the ECOA because the state "has primary and exclusive responsibility to pay for medical services given to Medicaid

---

[20] *See Chevron, U.S.A. v. Natural Resources Defense Council*, 467 U.S. 837, 844 (1984).

[21] Official Staff Commentary, 12 CFR 202.1(a)-1 (recognizing that the term "credit" under the ECOA is intentionally broader than the definition of "credit" under the Truth in Lending Act and applies to any "deferral of the payment of a debt.")

[22] Official Staff Commentary, 12 CFR 202.3.

[23] *See* 467 U.S. at 844.

[24] Fair Credit Reporting Medical Information Regulations, 70 Fed. Reg. 70666 (Nov. 22, 2005).

[25] 902 F. Supp. 139, 141 & n.3 (S.D. Ohio 1995).

patients,"[26] the court stated as follows: "The ECOA does not discuss whether medical service providers can be creditors, but the Federal Reserve Board categorizes delayed billing for medical services as a type of credit."[27] Similarly, one recent legal treatise on the subject explains that "[b]ecause credit under the ECOA involves any simple deferral of payment, even if there are no finance charges or installments, the ECOA applies to many transactions where the consumer pays after receiving the goods or services, such as doctor and hospital bills, bills from repair persons and other workers, and even a local store where a customer runs up a tab."[28]

This interpretation of "creditor" to include certain health care providers is consistent with the broad anti-discrimination purpose behind the ECOA. The law was intended to eradicate discrimination in all credit-related situations, including the deferral of payments for medical products or services.

Accordingly, based on the authority cited above, the FTC staff believes that professionals, including physicians, who regularly bill their clients, customers, or patients for their services after those services are rendered, are "creditors" under the ECOA. Indeed, Congress would need to exclude physicians explicitly from FACTA's definition of creditor for them to be excluded from the Red Flags Rule.

You suggest that physicians do not view themselves as creditors under the ECOA because they submit claims to health insurance carriers. This fact, however, does not change the fundamental credit aspects of the transaction.[29] When a physician submits a claim to an insurance carrier first and then bills any remaining unpaid amounts to the patient – whether she does so as a courtesy to the patient or because she is required to do so as a matter of contractual or state law – the physician is deferring the consumer's payment of his or her share of the claim (i.e., the physician is billing the patient <u>after</u> having provided the patient with medical services). Indeed, in many such instances, patients provide written acknowledgment that they are responsible for any amounts unpaid by insurance when they enter into a relationship with a physician. Moreover, as a matter of sound business practice, physicians typically avail themselves of their full rights to pursue unpaid bills, including reporting medical debts to consumer reporting agencies. Thus, although the primary responsibility of physicians is to provide health care, they also are conducting a business – a business that provides services for which payment may be deferred.

---

[26] *Id.* at 141.

[27] *Id.* at 141, n.3. *Cf., Williams*, 5 F. Supp. 2d at 1145 (looking to the Official Staff Commentary of Regulation B in holding that the plaintiff's application for cellular telephone service constituted credit because it involved "the purchase of services and deferral of payment for those services.")

[28] Theodore Eisenberg, 1-5 Debtor-Creditor Law § 5.02 (Matthew Bender & Co., Inc., 2008).

[29] *Mick v. Level Propane Gases, Inc.*, 183 F. Supp. 2d 1014 (S.D. Ohio 2000) (The court found that in determining whether an entity is a "creditor" under the ECOA, "[i]t is the nature of the service transaction at issue that is determinative.")

**Figure 7.2.** FTC letter to the American Medical Association on red flag applicability *(continued)*

In further support of your position that physicians are not creditors, in your letter you cite to *Riethman v. Berry*,[30] a case involving the issue of whether a law firm was an ECOA creditor. Although the court found that the defendant attorneys were not creditors under the ECOA, the *Riethman* court did not cite or refer to the Official Staff Commentary of Regulation B. This omission is significant because, as discussed above, this Official Commentary explicitly includes lawyers and physicians within the definition of incidental creditor for purposes of the ECOA, and these conclusions should be granted substantial deference.

You also rely on *Shaumyan v. Sidetex Co.*[31] This case is not factually relevant to the issue of whether physicians who defer payment for medical services are creditors under the ECOA. *Shaumyan* involved a home improvement contract that provided for the plaintiffs to make an initial deposit and then additional payments as the work progressed, with payment for the total cost of the contracted work due upon completion of the work.[32] The court held that this arrangement was not a credit transaction under the ECOA because it did not involve deferred payment for work; instead, it involved incremental, "substantially contemporaneous" payments made as the work progressed.[33] Unlike the facts presented in *Shaumyan*, it is our understanding that physicians generally do not bill patients in increments as work progresses; to the contrary, they bill patients after the services have been completed, sometimes allowing patients to pay in installments. This type of delayed payment is not the type of "substantially contemporaneous" payment at issue in *Shaumyan*.

Finally, you assert that physicians who bill for services after the services are rendered are not creditors under the Red Flags Rule because health care providers were not explicitly referenced in the Rule "among the trades or businesses identified as creditors." Although it is true that health care providers are not enumerated in the short list of examples, that does not lead to the conclusion that such practitioners are not covered. The listed examples were not intended to be exhaustive, but merely illustrative, as indicated by the statement that the term "includes" the enumerated businesses.[34]

### Developing Appropriate Programs for Physicians

You have asserted that physicians should not have to comply with the Red Flags Rule because they have devoted substantial resources to complying with HIPAA's

---

[30] 287 F.3d 274 (3d Cir. 2002).

[31] 900 F.2d 16 (2d Cir. 1990).

[32] *Id.* at 17.

[33] *Id.* at 18.

[34] *See Puerto Rico Maritime Shipping Auth. v. ICC*, 645 F.2d 1102, 1112 n.26 (D.C. Cir. 1981) ("It is hornbook law that the use of the word 'including' indicates that the specified list . . . that follows is illustrative, not exclusive.") (citation omitted)).

privacy and security requirements and because they maintain an ethical obligation to protect patient confidentiality. This argument misapprehends the purpose and application of the Red Flags Rule. We certainly recognize the importance of HIPAA's privacy and security requirements and the essential role data security plays in protecting individuals' health information from compromise and misuse, as well as physicians' ethical responsibilities in this area. But, notwithstanding physicians' reasonable efforts to prevent them from doing so, identity thieves have a variety of means of obtaining personal information. A comprehensive approach to combating medical identity theft, therefore, must include measures aimed not only at preventing the compromise of patient information, but also at preventing or mitigating the misuse of that information if it is compromised. The Rule is designed to prevent identity theft primarily by ensuring that organizations are alert to signs that an identity thief is using someone else's identifying information fraudulently to obtain products or services, including services such as medical care. Thus, the Red Flags Rule generally complements rather than duplicates the HIPAA data security requirements.

In meeting with you, and in your correspondence, you noted your concerns about the impact of the Red Flags Rule on the practice of medicine, including concerns that physicians will begin to demand payment up front or abandon the practice of medicine altogether. We are, of course, sensitive to the concern that the Rule requirements could be burdensome for health care providers, potentially leading to unintended costs for consumers.

Given the risk-based nature of the Rule's requirements, as a practical matter, however, we do not believe that the Rule would impose significant burdens for most providers. As discussed above, the Red Flags Rule is designed to be flexible and tailored to the degree of identity theft risk faced by the particular physician; in many cases, that risk may be minimal or non-existent, such that a simple and streamlined program would be adequate. For example, for most physicians in a low risk environment, an appropriate program might consist of checking a photo identification at the time services are sought and having appropriate procedures in place in the event the office is notified – say by a consumer or law enforcement – that the consumer's identity has been misused. Such procedures might include not trying to collect the debt from the true consumer or not reporting it on the consumer's credit report, as well as ensuring that any medical information about the identity thief is maintained separately from information about the consumer. These types of simple practices are already becoming more commonplace in many physicians' offices.

As you are aware, the Commission recently granted entities subject to its jurisdiction a six-month forbearance period before it will begin enforcement of the Rule. This action was taken in light of the fact that a number of industries and professions had been unaware of their coverage by and responsibilities under the Rule. In the meantime, FTC staff has continued its outreach efforts to help covered entities come into compliance with the Rule, including working with a number of trade associations that have chosen to develop model policies or specialized guidance for their members.

**Figure 7.2.   FTC letter to the American Medical Association on red flag applicability** *(continued)*

      FTC staff would be pleased to assist the AMA in helping its members to comply with the Red Flags Rule in the least burdensome manner possible. We are also willing to work with the AMA to ensure that physicians are receiving accurate information about the Rule to counteract any misinformation that may be circulating from other sources. We believe that a collaborative approach of this sort could be highly effective in helping physicians minimize the occurrence and consequences of medical identity theft.

      Sincerely,

      Eileen Harrington
      Acting Director of Bureau of Consumer Protection

Source: FTC 2009.

- Methods to foster the public understanding of HIT

- Strategies to enhance the use of HIT in improving the quality of healthcare, reducing medical errors, reducing health disparities, improving public health, increasing prevention and coordination with community resources, and improving the continuity of care among health care settings

- Specific plans for ensuring that populations with unique needs, such as children, are appropriately addressed in the technology design, as appropriate, which may include technology that automates enrollment and retention for eligible individuals

The third and fourth bullets in this make it clear that the HIT Policy Committee will be influencing national health information privacy policy substantially over the next few years.

Membership of the HIT Policy Committee is comprised of three individuals chosen by the HHS Secretary, 13 members appointed by the Acting Comptroller General of the United States, and four members appointed by the Majority and Minority Leaders of the Senate and the Speaker and Minority Leader of the House of Representatives. The Committee is chaired by David Blumenthal, MD, National Coordinator for Health Information Technology.

Some of the group's earliest work centered on defining the "meaningful use" language within ARRA's incentive provisions for adoption of electronic health records. Although the focus on that discussion is beyond just privacy and security issues, those topics did figure prominently in the list of "Health Outcomes Policy Priorities" that the group recommended be part of the criteria for "meaningful use." A link to the matrix that lists these policy priorities can be found on the HIT Policy Committee's Web site, listed on the CD-ROM accompanying this book.

## eHealth Initiative Blueprint: Principles on Managing Privacy, Security, and Confidentiality

The *eHealth Initiative Blueprint: Building Consensus for Common Action* (2007) is the result of multi-stakeholder consensus on a shared vision and a set of principles, strategies, and actions for improving health and healthcare through information and information technology. Development of the Blueprint involved nearly 200 organizations representing the diversity of stakeholders in healthcare, including clinicians, consumers, employers and healthcare purchasers, healthcare IT suppliers, health plans, hospitals and other providers, laboratories, the life sciences industry, pharmacies, public health agencies, and state and regional leaders. The Blueprint is designed to offer guidance to a wide range of audiences, not strictly those organizations covered by ARRA or HIPAA. In this way, the principles are designed to benefit organizations operating in every sector of healthcare and may be of increasing value in the future as the scope of privacy and security protections for health information expands.

A part of that Blueprint focused specifically on privacy, security, and confidentiality principles and those are listed in figure 7.3.

### Figure 7.3.   eHealth Initiative Blueprint: Privacy, Security, and Confidentiality Principles

1. **Transparency**

    - Policies for the permissible use of personal health information by those other than the patient should be clearly defined, accessible, and communicated in an easily understood format.

    - Individuals have the right to know how their personal health information has been used and who has access to it.

2. **Collection and Use of Personal Health Information**

    - Personal health information of the individual consumer should be obtainable consistent with applicable federal, state, and local law. It should be accurate, up-to-date, and limited to what is appropriate and relevant for the intended use.

    - Consumers have a right to privacy of their personal health information, taking into account existing exceptions under law. Consumers should be apprised when they have a choice in how their personal health information will be used and shared and when they can limit uses of their personal health information.

3. **Individual Control**

    - Individuals should be able to limit when and with whom their identifiable personal health information is shared. Individuals should be able to delegate these responsibilities to another person.

- Individuals should be able to readily obtain an audit trail that discloses by whom their personal health information has been accessed and how it has been used.

4. **Security**
   - Measures should be implemented to protect the integrity, security, and confidentiality of each individual's personal health information, ensuring that it cannot be lost, stolen, or accessed or modified in an inappropriate way.
   - Organizations that store, transmit, or use personal health information should have in place mechanisms for authentication and authorization of system users.

5. **Audit**
   - Each such organization must have a comprehensive audit process to examine compliance with its internal privacy, security, and confidentiality policies and procedures.
   - Organizations have a responsibility to ensure that an individual is notified when the organization learns of unauthorized or inappropriate access to that individual's personal health information.

6. **Accountability and Oversight**
   - Individuals should be apprised as to who monitors policy compliance with privacy, security, and confidentiality policies, how complaints will be handled, how individuals will be informed of a violation and existing remedies available to them.

7. **Technology and Privacy**
   - Technological developments must be adopted in harmony with policies and business rules that foster trust and transparency.
   - Privacy protections must be at the forefront of all technological standards. Privacy issues cannot be addressed post-system design and implementation.

Source: eHealth Initiative Blueprint 2007; Excerpted with permission.

## The Markle Foundation's Connecting for Health Project

Begun in 2002, Connecting for Health is a public–private collaborative designed to address barriers to the development of an interconnected health information infrastructure. The first phase of the Collaborative's work included developing consensus on the adoption of an initial set of data standards, case studies on privacy, and security and helped define the electronic PHR. More recently, Connecting for Health developed recommendations on the near-term actions necessary to achieving electronic connectivity in healthcare.

Over the life of Connecting for Health, the project has published a wide variety of resources on privacy and security. One of those sets of resources is mentioned here, because of its focus on the

# Policy Efforts Impacting the Privacy Rules of ARRA

role and rights of the consumer with respect to networked personal health information. These resources are mentioned here, and they (along with many more) can be accessed on the Web. They are also listed in appendix B on the CD-ROM that accompanies this book.

*Connecting Consumers: Common Framework for Networked Personal Health Information* (also known as *the Framework*) is a multi-part framework proposing a set of practices that, when taken together, encourage appropriate handling of personal health information as it flows to and from PHRs and similar applications or supporting services (Markle Foundation 2008–2009). It is intended to offer a foundation for maintaining trust among all the participants in electronic health information networks.

The framework proposes enabling consumers to have ready access to electronic copies of their personal health information, including their own contributions, under a set of "fair information practices" that respect the consumer's preferences for how their information is collected and shared. The term *networked* refers to connectivity of health information across organizational boundaries.

The Framework includes proposed practices in the following "consumer policy" areas:

- Policy overview
- Policy notice to consumers
- Consumer consent to collections, uses, and disclosures of information
- Chain of trust agreements
- Notification of misuse or breach
- Dispute resolution
- Discrimination and compelled disclosures
- Consumer obtainment and control of information
- Enforcement of policies

The project also has published proposed practices with respect to information technology affecting consumers:

- Technology overview
- Authentication of consumers
- Immutable audit trails
- Limitations on identifying information
- Portability of information
- Security and systems requirements

- Architecture for consumer participation

These are not the only resources from Connecting for Health that touch on privacy and security matters. Additional resources can be freely downloaded from their Web site, listed in appendix B on the CD-ROM.

## Other Organizations and Collaborations

The initiatives and groups listed earlier are the proverbial tip of the iceberg when it comes to groups focused on health information privacy and security. The HIT Standards Committee of the ONC (and mandated by Section 3003 of ARRA) will be instrumental in recommending standards, implementation specifications, and certification criteria for the exchange of electronic health information and will be coordinating their efforts with the HIT Policy Committee already discussed. ONC also will be appointing a privacy official to coordinate and help lead their ongoing work on privacy.

The National eHealth Collaborative, as the successor organization to the original American Health Information Community (AHIC) formed by HHS, is a public–private partnership to continue the health IT standards development work begun under AHIC. However, given the mandate of an HIT Standards Committee, the role of this group in standards development is not yet certain.

In addition to these, a number of other national groups have a strong focus on the development of health information privacy and security resources, notably American Health Information Management Association (AHIMA), AMIA (American Medical Informatics Association), Center for Democracy and Technology's Health Privacy Project, Healthcare Information and Management Systems Society (HIMSS), and the World Privacy Forum, among others. Associated Web URLs are provided on the book's CD-ROM.

Clearly, the health information privacy landscape is changing. Not only will the healthcare industry see ongoing regulations and guidance from the federal government, but private organizations such as some of those described here will also continue to influence the direction of our national privacy policy as we move forward. Changes like those in the form of legislation, such as ARRA and regulations from HHS and others, create challenges for the organizations and individuals creating, using, accessing, and disclosing protected health information. Meeting such challenges is necessary not only as a compliance strategy, but as an inevitable part of the process of adequately protecting health information while the nation seeks to improve care and reduce costs through the use of that information.

## References

American Recovery and Reinvestment Act of 2009. Public Law 111-5.

Department of Health and Human Services. 2008. *The Nationwide Privacy and Security Framework for Electronic Exchange of Individually Identifiable Health Information.* http://healthit.hhs.gov/portal/server.pt?open=512&mode=2&cached=true&objID=1173.

eHealth Initiative. 2007. *eHI Blueprint–Building Consensus for Common Action.* Washington, D.C.: eHealth Initiative.

Federal Trade Commission. 2009 (February 4). Letter to Margaret Garikes of the American Medical Association. http://www.ftc.gov/os/statutes/redflags.pdf.

Federal Trade Commission. 2009 (August 25). Final rule: Health breach notification rule. *Federal Register.*

Markle Foundation. 2008–2009. *Connecting Consumers: Common Framework for Networked Personal Health Information.* New York, NY: Markle Foundation.

# Appendix A

# Frequently Asked Questions

## General Questions

*Q: Where can I find the actual ARRA legislation?*

*A:* http://www.thomas.gov/home/approp/app09.html#h1. The privacy provisions of ARRA can also be found in a PDF on the book's CD-ROM.

*Q: What is the difference between ARRA and HITECH?*

*A:* HITECH is part of ARRA. The American Recovery and Reinvestment Act (ARRA) is officially Public Law 111-5 and was signed on February 17, 2009 by President Barack Obama. ARRA provides many different stimulus opportunities, one of which is $19.2 billion on HIT. Title XIII of ARRA has the subtitle: Health Information Technology for Economic and Clinical Health Act (HITECH). It is this section (ARRA, 112–165) that deals with many of the health information communication and technology provisions including Subpart D–Privacy (ARRA, 144–165).

*Q: I work at a hospital. Do I have to make sure my business associates are meeting their privacy and security requirements?*

*A:* There's nothing that forces you to make sure they are meeting their obligations, but remember, under HIPAA's Privacy Rule you have obligations to act when a business associate of yours is violating the applicable rules—either by making sure they have addressed the problem, or if they can't or won't, by terminating the agreement. Most CEs will likely want to be sure that their BAs are holding up their end of the business associate agreement, at the very least.

*Q: If there's a problem with privacy where I work (covered entity), can I be personally liable?*

*A:* In some limited circumstances. HHS has made it clear that individuals can be criminally liable in some limited circumstances, and in fact we've already seen some criminal prosecutions (generally they have involved individuals who have breached a patient's privacy for financial gain).

Neither HIPAA nor ARRA allow individuals to file civil suits for privacy breaches, but civil suits can sometimes be pursued under state law. Ordinarily, as long as you are acting within the scope of your authority at work, the employer is responsible for your behavior.

*Q: I can't get our leadership to commit resources to start our ARRA/HITECH compliance efforts. Any suggestions?*

*A:* Check out an article by LaVonne Wieland of AHIMA, in the October 2009 "In Confidence" column in the *Journal of AHIMA*. It offers some practical advice on securing leadership support. Circulating articles about the regulations, and suggested compliance strategies, can also be a good way of getting attention for the need for compliance resources.

*Q: Where can I find a Web page for comprehensive information related to ARRA?*

*A:* http://www.ahima.org/arra/ and see the other links on the CD-ROM included with this book. This particular link is to AHIMA's ARRA page, an ongoing, updated list of resources.

*Q: Where can I find AHIMA's analysis of ARRAs impact on privacy?*

*A:* http://www.ahima.org/dc/documents/AnalysisofARRAPrivacy-fin-3-2009a.pdf

*Q: Where can I find a list of important ARRA dates?*

*A:* http://www.ahima.org/dc/documents/AHIMAReviewofARRARequiredReports.pdf is the direct link to the AHIMA summary of important dates with respect to privacy. Those dates are also summarized in table 3.1 (chapter 3).

*Q: Where can I find AHIMA's ARRA Web page?*

*A:* http://www.ahima.org/arra

*Q: Where can I find HHS security guidance?*

*A:* HHS released guidance for HIPAA-covered entities in the April 27, 2009 *Federal Register* (74FR19006).

*Q: I work for a business associate. Where can I find FTC Security Guidance?*

*A:* Careful! Business associates are subject to the HHS security regulations and are *not* subject to the FTC rules on breaches of security of PHR to the extent they are acting as a business associate for a covered entity.

*Q: What provisions exist for updates to the ARRA privacy law provisions and guidance documents once released? Will it be like HIPAA with no changes or updates over time?*

*A:* HHS is expected to release a series of guidance documents and implementing regulations over the next several years and could update those annually. There are likely to be many changes over the next several years. The timeline of key dates mentioned earlier shows various expected dates for additional regulations and guidance.

Appendix A

# Breaches

*Q: Where can the breach notification regulations be found?*

A: The HHS interim final rule on breach notification, which applies to covered entities and business associates, was published in the August 24, 2009 Federal Register. The FTC final rule on breaches involving PHR information was published on August 25, 2009, in the Federal Register. Copies of both can be found on the CD-ROM accompanying this book.

*Q: What are the effective dates of the breach notification rules?*

A: Both the HHS and FTC rules take effect 30 days after publication; meaning September 23, 2009, for the HHS rule and September 24, 2009, for the FTC rule. Be aware that HHS has announced plans to delay enforcement of their rule for the first six months after publication (meaning penalties will not be assessed), however, the rules are still effective on the dates noted earlier.

*Q: As a covered entity, do we need to follow both the HHS and FTC rules?*

A: No, the HHS rules are for covered entities and business associates. The FTC breach rules apply to noncovered entities with PHR information. Refer to chapter 6 for a more complete explanation of applicability.

Q: If a reportable breach occurs at a business associate, when does the 60-day reporting deadline actually begin—is it when the breach occurs, or when the covered entity knows about it?

A: The answer depends in part on the role that business associate plays in relation to the covered entity. If the business associate is truly an agent of the covered entity, the CE's knowledge will be considered to have occurred when the agent/business associate knew (or reasonably should have known) of the breach. So, the latest date for reporting will be 60 days from when the BA knew or should have known. However, the more common relationship is one of independent contractor, If the relationship is one of an independent contractor, the covered entity's obligation to report is within 60 days of when that breach is known (or should have been known) by the covered entity,, and in most cases that will mean when the breach has been reported to the covered entity by the business associate. It is important to note that for those situations where the business associate is acting as an "agent" of the covered entity, rapid reporting will be essential, and the covered entity may want to impose much more rapid reporting deadlines on those business associates. Legal counsel will be helpful in distinguishing between "agents" and "independent contractors."

*Q: Do the breach notification requirements apply to incidental disclosures as defined by the Privacy Rule?*

A: No. As long as the disclosure qualifies as an incidental disclosure under the Privacy Rule, it does not qualify as a *breach* under the HHS definition.

*Q: Do breach notification obligations apply if only one patient's information is breached?*

A: Yes. The number of patients involved is only relevant to the types of notifications required. Refer to chapter 2 for a deeper discussion of additional requirements for breaches involving larger numbers of patients.

*Q: Is a staff member who inappropriately accesses patient information committing a breach?*

*A:* They are violating the Privacy Rule, which is one element of the definition of breach. But for that access to be a breach requiring notification, all elements of the definition must be met. In this case, the access must also compromise the security or privacy of the information. Whether that element is met requires a risk assessment that considers whether there is a significant risk of financial, reputational, or other harm to the individual whose information was accessed. In any event, this action should result in appropriate disciplinary action.

*Q: Can I just e-mail the breach notification to a patient?*

*A:* No; you must send notification by first class mail; but you may also use e-mail notification if the patient wishes you to contact him or her that way.

*Q: One of my business associates (BA) had a breach. Do I have to do anything, as a covered entity?*

*A:* If that breach involved PHI from your organization, the BA must notify you and supply certain information. You'll then use that information and the results of your own risk analysis to determine whether breach notification of the patient (and potentially others) is required under the rules. See chapter 2 for more information.

*Q: What constitutes due diligence with breach notification? If a letter notification is mailed to the only address a covered entity has on record and it comes back undeliverable, is that due diligence?*

*A:* That's the first step, but only the first step. The August 24, 2009 breach regulations from HHS provide a description of additional "substitute notice" steps you may need to take, depending on the number of persons whose information was breached. Forms of substitute notice can include written notification to the next of kin or personal representative (unless you have insufficient or out-of-date contact information for those parties), telephone notice if fewer than 10 individuals, a conspicuous 90-day posting on your organization's Web site home page if 10 or more individuals are involved, or notice to major print or broadcast media in geographic areas where the individuals affected by the breach likely reside, and there are additional provisions for urgent situations and larger breaches. See the Substitute Notice provisions in Section 164.404(d)(2).

*Q: Is there a special form covered entities must use in reporting breaches to HHS?*

*A:* Yes; the notification must be made electronically, completing the electronic form which can be found on the HHS privacy Web page: www.hhs.gov/ocr/privacy/hipaa/administrative/breachnotificationrule/brinstruction.html.

## Accounting of Disclosures

*Q: Will all TPO (treatment, payment, healthcare operations) disclosures now be subject to the accounting of disclosures?*

*A:* No; the expanded obligations for TPO disclosure reporting only apply to organizations using or maintaining an electronic health record. And the obligation appears to apply only to those TPO disclosures made through an electronic health record. See chapter 2 for a full discussion of this, and be aware that this issue is being interpreted in various ways while the industry awaits HHS guidance.

*Q: Must breaches be tracked on the accounting of disclosures?*

*A:* Not necessarily; the answer will depend on a couple of factors. The general rule is that all disclosures must be tracked unless they meet one of the exceptions listed in the Privacy Rule. The HIPAA exception for TPO disclosures has now been narrowed, as noted in the answer above. Whether a breach must be tracked will depend on whether it involved a "disclosure"—not all breaches will involve disclosures. For example, an improper internal use of information could well constitute a breach under the rule, but not qualify as a disclosure. Assuming it is an actual disclosure, it will be subject to tracking on the accounting unless it meets one of the original HIPAA exceptions, as modified by ARRA for organizations using electronic health records. Keep in mind, however, that if you have a breach requiring patient notification, and it is *not* listed on the accounting that the patient may request, this could be a source of some confusion and suspicion. If that is a concern, there is nothing to prevent you from accounting for all breaches, whether they technically qualify or not.

## Patient Rights and Requests

*Q: Do I have to give the patient an electronic copy of their health information? What if that's not easily done with our software?*

*A:* As of the February 18, 2010 compliance date for this provision, you will, if that information is in electronic form. HIPAA also required this if the information was readily reproducible in electronic format, but we are still awaiting clarifying guidance and regulations from HHS. So now is the time to begin speaking with your vendor about their plans for adding this functionality.

*Q: We never accept patient requests for restrictions on the use/disclosure of their information. Is this still acceptable?*

*A:* No; if that request seeks to withhold PHI from a health plan for non-treatment-related disclosures and the patient has fully paid for the service or item (to which the PHI pertains) out of pocket. For other types of restriction requests, the covered entity still has some flexibility in deciding whether they can reasonably and reliably accommodate that restriction request. Keep in mind, when evaluating whether or not a disclosure to an insurer is "treatment-related," that the deciding factor is the purpose of the disclosure to the insurer. Disclosures purely for case management purposes would be considered treatment-related, but the majority of disclosures to insurers are payment-related, not treatment-related.

*Q: Do I have to share audit trails of employee access to a patient's electronic record if the patient requests it?*

*A:* ARRA does not require the sharing of actual audit trails; however, breach notification regulations may necessitate the sharing of certain information that can be found on that audit trail. Keep in mind, however, that some covered entities do choose to voluntarily share information about employee accesses if a patient has a specific concern.

*Q: Does ARRA affect the HIPAA time limits for responding to patients' requests for their health information?*

*A:* No, those time limits still apply.

*Q: My state has defined allowable copying costs. Is this affected by ARRA?*

*A:* It may be. The answer will depend on whether you can comply with both sets of requirements, or whether the state law is considered "contrary" to ARRA's provisions. ARRA is silent as to paper copies, but has provisions to limit costs associated with requests for PHI in electronic format.

## Business Associates and Business Associate Agreements

*Q: Do I have to amend all existing business associate agreements (BAAs)?*

*A:* This is currently under debate in a variety of circles. ARRA does appear to require incorporation of the new business associate obligations into the BAA. Some lawyers, however, believe that this can be done automatically if the current BAA includes broad language as to the business associate's agreement to comply with all applicable current and "future" laws. This is a question best discussed with your own legal counsel, as the approach has implications for not only the covered entity's regulatory compliance, but also its ability to exercise oversight of its business associates .

*Q: We plan to amend our business associate agreements. Can we do this as they naturally come up for renewal, or do we have to do them all at once?*

*A:* Those changes will need to be incorporated by no later than the compliance date of this portion of the law: February 18, 2010. It is important to note, however, that certain business associate obligations will take effect prior to 2010—for example, breach notification to the covered entity. So there are good reasons to incorporate those obligations earlier, in line with any associated effective dates prior to February 2010.

*Q: Does HHS offer a recommended, or model, business associate agreement?*

*A:* They did offer model language when the privacy rule was first published. As of press date, there is no official updated model agreement from HHS.

*Q: I work for a covered entity. Do we have to make sure my business associates are meeting their privacy and security requirements?*

*A:* See the third Q&A under the General Provisions section of this appendix.

## Staff Education

*Q: Who must be trained about the new requirements, and when?*

*A:* In short, your workforce members who are affected by the requirements. That will be a long list. And there are excellent reasons to include at least some basic ARRA information in training for all workforce members because of the risk of criminal liability. As was true under HIPAA, you can and should tailor the training to the role of the recipient. You will want to complete initial training in advance of the effective dates for compliance, so staff will not unknowingly violate provisions of the law or regulations.

*Q: Is a covered entity responsible for training non-employed medical staff members?*

*A:* They are part of your workforce, have access to PHI, and should be trained by the covered entity.

*Q: Is a covered entity responsible for training business associates?*

*A:* No; but there may be situations in which you wish to offer some training. For example, if a BA is going to be newly responsible for accounting for their own disclosures, you may wish to help them understand how that should dovetail with your own approach. Or you may wish to train them in exactly how you wish to be notified of breaches by the business associates. But you are under no obligation to train business associates.

*Q: Are there any requirements for periodic retraining about privacy and security?*

*A:* HIPAA has always required updating the training for applicable workforce members when making changes to privacy procedures and policies that affect those workforce members.

*Q: Should we require our staff to sign an acknowledgement that they participated in training and agree to follow the rules?*

*A:* This is not mandatory, but it can be a useful element of documentation in showing your own good faith in educating your workforce to follow the rules. It can also be useful in supporting disciplinary actions, if necessary.

*Q: Should I use prepackaged training programs/videos for our staff training? Is that sufficient?*

*A:* These can be useful for generic education, but it's best to supplement that training with information specific to your organization and its policies and procedures. See the warning about "canned" materials, including policies and procedures, in chapter 4, Implementation Strategies.

# Index

Access control policies and procedures, 15–16
Accounting of disclosures
    by business associate, 40, 46
    EHR to develop, 10, 17–18, 26–27
    frequently asked questions for, 92–93
Administrative safeguards
    applicable to business associates, 12–14
    for individually identifiable health information, 69, 70
Advisory Committee on Automated Personal Data Systems, 62–63
American Health Information Community (AHIC), formation of, 3
American Health Information Management Association (AHIMA)
    analysis of ARRA by, 10
    ARRA/HITECH compliance recommendations of, 90
    ARRA Web page of, 90
    initiatives for protecting health information of, 2
    Web site for ARRA of, 90
American Medical Association (AMA), FTC letter on red flag rules to, 73, 74–82
American Reinvestment and Recovery Act of 2009 (ARRA). *See also* Health Information Technology for Economic and Clinical Health Act (HITECH) provisions of ARRA
    access rights for obtaining health information in electronic format under, 10, 18, 25–26
    accounting for disclosures through EHR under, 10, 17–18, 26–27
    breach defined in, 20–23, 56, 57
    breach notification requirements of, 9, 11, 19–24, 31, 39–40, 49
    business associate provisions of, 9, 11–19
    conditions for marketing and fundraising contacts of, 28–30
    effective dates for, 18, 37–39, 46, 90
    enforcement provisions of, 19, 30–31
    focus of, 3–5, 6
    frequently asked questions about, 89–90
    guidance documents for, 90
    healthcare privacy issues of, list of, 9–10
    impact beyond HIPAA of, 51–54
    implementation strategies for, 43–50
    incentive payments to physicians and hospitals under Title IV, Section 4101 of, 4, 5
    parties affected by, 5–6
    passage of, 1
    penalties under, 18, 30, 31
    policy efforts affecting, 61–87
    restrictions on disclosures of health information under, requests for, 24–25, 41, 49–50
    restrictions on sale of health information under, 9, 17, 25, 38
    scope of, 9
    text of, accessing, 89
    unresolved questions and conflicts for, 55–60
Audit trails of employee access to electronic records, 94
Authentication, person or entity, 16

Best practices for treatment disclosures, 39
Breach, definition of
    ARRA, 20–23, 31–32, 56, 57
    CFR, 20–22, 56–57
    exceptions to, 20–21, 58–59
Breach log, annual submission of, 22
Breach notification provisions of ARRA, 9, 19–24
    deadlines for, 11, 21
    *Federal Register* publication of, 91
    for FTC, 51
    individual notification requirements in, 21–22, 49
    policies and procedures revised for, 21, 39–40
Breach notification requirement of HHS and FTC
    due diligence for, 92
    effective dates of, 91
    *Federal Register* publication of, 23, 72–73
    not applied to incidental disclosure, 91
Breaches of unsecured PHI, larger scale, 22, 91
Business associate agreements (BAAs)
    ARRA expansion of liability incorporated in, 18
    model, 94
    revisions to, 41–42, 59–60, 94
Business associate contracting strategy, 46–47
Business associates
    accounting of disclosures by, 40, 46
    ARRA provisions for, 5, 9, 11–19, 42
    covered entity response to breach by, 92
    disclosures by, 11, 17–18
    need for new or revised policies and procedures of, 40–41
    referrals by covered entities to, 27
    reportable beach occurring at, reporting deadline for, 91
    training for, 95

Change management process, 43–50
    guiding, 44–45
    steps in, 43
Chief Privacy Officer for ONC, 37
Civil penalties for noncompliance with HIPAA, 18–19
Civil suits for privacy breaches, 89–90
Code of Fair Information Practice (1973), 63, 66
Compliance with ARRA and HIPAA, report to Congress on, 39

Compliance with ARRA rules, 6–7, 39
    preparation for, 41
Compliance with HIPAA privacy and security regulations, review of, 47
*Connecting Consumers: Common Framework for Networked Personal Health Information* (Framework), 85
Connecting for Health project (Markle Foundation), 2, 84–86
Copying costs, defined allowable, 94
Covered entities
    accounting of disclosures by, 10, 17, 26–27
    ARRA changes affecting, 5
    availability of PHI from, 25, 41
    defined under HIPAA, 2
    disclosure of PHI by person at, 20
    HHS rules for, 91
    liability of, 89–90
    noncompliance reporting by, 19
    referrals by, 27
    restriction requests handled by, 93
    preemption analyses by, 42
Criminal penalties for noncompliance with HIPAA, 18
CVS Casemark, FTC case against, 52–53

Data integrity policies and procedures, 16
Deidentified data, 10
Department of Health and Human Services (HHS)
    ARRA guidance documents by, 23, 30, 37, 38, 90
    breach notification methodology of, 12
    breach notification requirements of, 20, 91
    education initiatives of, 38
    Privacy Rule (2000) of, 2
    privacy Web page of, 92
    regional privacy advisors in, 9
    reports to Congress by, 10
Documentation of decision-making process for ARRA/HITECH implementation, 44–45
Documentation of training, usefulness of, 95
Documentation requirements for business associates, 16–18
Documents, retention requirements for, 48
Due diligence for breach notification, 92

# Index

Education programs
    ARRA Section 13403 provision for privacy, 32
    on breach of privacy and security, 46
    for business associates, 95
    on changes to HIPAA privacy and security regulations, subgroups for, 35–37
    on health information privacy, OCR initiative for, 32
    prepackaged, 95
    on uses of health information, 9
    workforce, 35, 49, 95
*eHealth Initiative Blueprint: Building Consensus for Common Action* (Blueprint), 83–84
Electronic health records (EHRs)
    acceptance of safety concerns in, 6
    accounting for disclosures for covered entities that use, 10, 17–18, 26–27
    availability and usage of, 54
    certified, 4
    difficulties in implementing, 6
    incentive provisions for adoption of, 82
    for tracking disclosures, 47
Electronic information exchange, 4
Electronic medical records
    providing patients with selected health information from, 26
    public opinion of, 2
ePrescribing capability of certified EHR, 4

Federal Health IT Strategic Plan, 10
Federal Trade Commission (FTC)
    breach of security regulations issued by, 52, 91
    case against CVS Casemark of, 52–53
    Health Breach Notification Rule of, 20, 23, 72–73
    medical identity theft addressed in "red flag" program of, 73, 74–82
    Privacy Online by, 63
    reports to Congress by, 10, 63
    role in health information privacy and security of, 72–73
    security breach notifications by, 51–52
    Security Guidance of, 90
Federal Trade Commission Act, violations of requirements under, 23
Frequently asked questions
    for accounting of disclosures, 92–93
    for breach notification regulations, 91–92
    for business associations and business associate agreements, 94
    general privacy and security, 89–90
    for patient rights and requests, 93–94
    for staff education, 95
Fundraising contacts, PHI use for, 28–30
Fundraising, HIPAA Privacy Rules governing, 41

Grants and loan funding, agencies for, 4
Guidelines on the Protection of Privacy and Transborder Flows of Personal Data (OECD), 63

Health and Human Services (HHS), Department of. *See* Department of Health and Human Services (HHS)
Health information
    completeness and accuracy of, 69
    time limits for responding to patients' requests for, 94
Health information exchange organizations, 5
Health information privacy, activities of Congress on, 1
Health information privacy and security resources, organizations developing, 86
Health information technology (HIT), adoption of, 3, 6
Health information technology architecture, 4
Health Information Technology for Economic and Clinical Health Act (HITECH) provisions of ARRA
    effective dates for, 37–39, 46
    effects of, 1
    medical health information education programs under Section 3016 of, 4
    operational challenges of, 35–42
    overview of, 1–8
    scope of, 51
    as Title XIII of ARRA, 3–4, 89
Health Insurance Portability and Accountability Act (HIPAA)
    minimum necessary provisions of, 10, 27–28
    Privacy Rules of, 1, 9–33, 40, 55, 89

requests for restrictions on disclosures under, 24
Security Rules of, 1, 11, 55, 64
Health IT Regional Extension Centers, 4
Health plans, segregating health information disclosed to, 24–25
Healthcare operation, criteria for communication as, 29–30
Healthcare spending statistics, 3
HIT-listserv (American Health Lawyers Association), 55

Imaging studies, DVDs of, 25–26
Implementation strategies for HITECH Act changes, 43–50
    change management process in, steps of, 43
    changes to HIPAA privacy and security provisions of, 3
    guiding change process for, 44–45
    managers and staff involved in drafting, 45
    priorities of, 45–50
    risks of ARRA noncompliance minimized using, 3

Law enforcement, ARRA changes as affecting, 6
Limited data set, 27–28, 38

Marketing companies
    for healthcare clients, effects of ARRA on, 5, 10
    HIPAA Privacy Rules governing, 41
    "reasonable in amount" defined for, 38
    treatment of PHI by, 28–30
Markle Foundation, Connecting for Health project of, 84–86
Media, ARRA changes as affecting, 6

National eHealth Collaborative, 3, 86
National Institute for Standards and Technology (NIST), standards testing by, 4
Nationwide Privacy and Security Framework for Electronic Exchange of Individually Identifiable Health Information, 61–71
    accountability under, 70
    background of, 62–64

    collection, use, and disclosure limitation of, 68–69
    corrections of individually identifiable health information under, 67
    data quality and integrity under, 69
    glossary for, 70–71
    individual access under, 67
    individual choice under, 68
    methodology of, 64–65
    openness and transparency under, 68
    principles of, 65–67
    purpose of, 62
    safeguards under, 69
Noncovered entities
    ARRA HITECH provisions for, 10, 31–32
    breach of security by, 24
    FTC specification of breach notification requirements for, 23, 91
    privacy breach by, 2

Office of Civil Rights (OCR)
    corrective action by, 30
    national education initiative on uses of PHI by, 32
Office of the National Coordinator for Health Information Technology (ONC)
    authorization by HITECH of, 4
    chief privacy officer for, 10
    codification of, 9, 10
    duties of, 2–3, 9, 10–11
    establishment in 2004 of, 2, 10, 63
    HIT Policy Committee of, 11, 73, 82, 86
    HIT Standards Committee of, 11, 86
Operational challenges of HITECH changes to HIPAA regulations, 35–42

Penalties
    ARRA provisions for, 18, 30, 31
    distribution of, 39
Personal health information (PHI)
    baseline protections and safeguards for, 1
    data stewardship of electronic, 10
    electronic copy of, 25
    good faith belief of inability of recipient to retain, 59
    HHS rules for use or disclosure of, 20

# Index

inadvertent disclosure of, 58–59
incidental disclosures of, 91
OCR education program regarding uses of, 32
regulations on selling, 25
unintentional acquisition, access, or use of, 20, 58
Personal health record (PHR) systems
    commercial, 5
    consumer management of, 72
PHR identifiable health information, 24, 32
Physical safeguards
    applicable to business associates, 14–15
    for individually identifiable health information, 69, 71
Policies and procedures for implementing ARRA provisions
    availability to staff of, 48
    avoiding boilerplated, 48
    field-testing draft, 47–48
    need for, 40–41
Policy efforts affecting privacy rules of ARRA, 61–87
Preemption analysis
    for ARRA and state privacy laws, 42
    for HIPAA, 55
Privacy Act (1974), 63
Privacy advisors, HHS Secretary as appointing regional, 32
Privacy Rules (HIPAA), 1, 9–33
    accounting of disclosures under, 26
    as baseline standards, 64
    business associates subject to, 11, 59
    criticisms of, 5
    enforcement of, 10
    interpreting, 55
    limited data set under, 27–28
    obligations to act on violations of, 40, 89

Regulators, ARRA changes as affecting, 6
Requested restrictions on disclosures of health information, 24–25, 41, 45–50

Researchers, ARRA changes as affecting, 6
Retraining, updated programs for, 95
Risk assessment for breach under Privacy Rules, 92

Security Rules (HIPAA), 1
    as baseline standards, 64
    business associates subject to, 11
    interpreting, 55
State attorneys general, civil actions by, for HITECH violations, 54
State breach notification laws, 55–59
State privacy and security laws, 51, 63
Substitute notice steps under breach regulations, 92

Technical safeguards
    applied to business associates, 15–16
    for individually identifiable health information, 69, 71
Third-party service providers to vendors of PHRs, 23, 31, 41, 51
Transmission security measures, 16
Treatment, payment, healthcare operations (TPO) disclosures, 92–93

Unsecured protected health information, breach notification requirements applied to, 11–12

Vendors of PHRs, revised policies and procedures needed for, 40–41

Willful neglect regulations, 39
Workforce training, 35, 49, 95. *See also* Education programs